BASIC

lighthouse 2

Klassenarbeitstrainer

Deinen Klassenarbeitstrainer findest du auch in der **Cornelsen Lernen App**.

Siehst du eines dieser Symbole in deinem Klassenarbeitstrainer, findest du in der App …

🔊 alle **Audios**

▶ alle **Erklärfilme**

⬇ **Lösungen** zu den Aufgaben

Cornelsen

lighthouse 2 BASIC

Klassenarbeitstrainer

Im Auftrag des Verlages erarbeitet von
Marc Proulx, Berlin

In Zusammenarbeit mit der Englischredaktion
Klaus Unger (Projektleitung), Chelsea Ledvinka-Heß und
Elizabeth Pancake-Steeg, sowie Chiara Castellano

Beratende Mitwirkung
Katharina Pick, Wülfrath

Lizenzmanagement
Silke Kirchhoff

Illustrationen
Evelt Yanait, Advocate Art
Irina Zinner, Hamburg

Fotos
Anja Poehlmann, Brighton
Für die freundliche Unterstüzung danken wir der
Varndean School, Brighton

Umschlaggestaltung
Rosendahl, Berlin

Layoutkonzept
Klein & Halm, Berlin

Layout und technische Umsetzung
Compuscript Ireland and Chennai

Audio-Dateien
Studio
Clarity Studio, Berlin
Regie und Aufnahmeleitung
Susanne Kreutzer
Tontechnik
Dimitris Kritikos und Gislinde Böhringer

Druck
Athesiadruck GmbH, Bozen

PEFC-zertifiziert
Dieses Produkt
stammt aus
nachhaltig
bewirtschafteten
Wäldern und
kontrollierten Quellen

PEFC
PEFC/18-31-166   www.pefc.de

www.cornelsen.de

Soweit in diesem Lehrwerk Personen fotografisch abgebildet sind und ihnen von der Redaktion fiktive Namen, Berufe, Dialoge und Ähnliches zugeordnet oder diese Personen in bestimmte Kontexte gesetzt werden, dienen diese Zuordnungen und Darstellungen ausschließlich der Veranschaulichung und dem besseren Verständnis des Buchinhaltes.

Dieses Werk berücksichtigt die Regeln der reformierten Rechtschreibung und Zeichensetzung.

Die Webseiten Dritter, deren Internetadressen in diesem Lehrwerk angegeben sind, wurden vor Drucklegung sorgfältig geprüft. Der Verlag übernimmt keine Gewähr für die Aktualität und den Inhalt dieser Seiten oder solcher, die mit ihnen verlinkt sind.

Alle Drucke dieser Auflage sind inhaltlich unverändert und können im Unterricht nebeneinander verwendet werden.

1. Auflage, 1. Druck 2024
978-3-06-034595-3

Vorwort für Eltern

Sie möchten Ihrem Kind ein sicheres Gefühl für die Klassenarbeiten geben?
Der Klassenarbeitstrainer hilft Ihrem Kind beim Lernen.

Dear Parents,

in den Klassenarbeiten Ihrer Kinder werden die Fertigkeiten Hörverstehen (*Listening*), Leseverstehen (*Reading*), Wortschatz (*Words*), Grammatik (*Language*), Mediation, Lernen lernen (*Study skills*) und Schreiben (*Writing*) abgefragt. Mit dem Klassenarbeitstrainer kann Ihr Kind diese Fertigkeiten gezielt trainieren. Für jede Unit finden Sie verschiedene Aufgaben zu den einzelnen Fertigkeiten.

Im Klassenarbeitstrainer finden Sie darüber hinaus ein Kapitel mit Übungen zur Fertigkeit Sprechen (*Speaking*).

Vorbereitung

Nicht jedes Thema aus dem Schulbuch ist für jeden Lehrplan und für jedes Bundesland relevant, vergewissern Sie sich daher, dass Ihr Kind sich mindestens eine Woche vor der Klassenarbeit genau über die relevanten Themen informiert. Mit einem Lernplan kann Ihr Kind festlegen, wann welche Fertigkeit geübt wird. Eine Vorlage dafür finden Sie auf Seite 6.

More help-Aufgaben

Schreiben stellt für Schülerinnen und Schüler eine besondere Herausforderung dar. Das Kapitel *More help* stellt zusätzliche Hilfen (*useful phrases, switchboxes, etc.*) für die *Writing*-Aufgaben zur Verfügung.

Speaking-Aufgaben

Zwischen den Units 4 und 5 finden Sie Übungen zur Fertigkeit Sprechen (*Speaking*). Manche dieser Übungen kann Ihr Kind allein bearbeiten, andere am besten mit einem Partner (z. B. Klassenkameraden). Damit Sie die Ergebnisse mit den Lösungsvorschlägen vergleichen können, sollte sich Ihr Kind beim Sprechen aufnehmen. Beispielhafte Antworten werden in diesem Klassenarbeitstrainer auch als Audioformat zur Verfügung gestellt.

Lösungen

Wenn eine Aufgabe bearbeitet wurde, kann diese mit den Lösungen aus dem herausnehmbaren Lösungsheft verglichen werden. Achten Sie beim Vergleichen genau darauf, welche Fehler gemacht wurden, und überlegen Sie mit Ihrem Kind, wie diese beim nächsten Mal vermieden werden können. Neben den Beispiellösungen enthält das Lösungsheft auch Lerntipps und die Skripte zu den Hörtexten. Die Bewertungstabelle am Ende jeder Unit hilft Ihnen dabei, den Lernstand Ihres Kindes besser einschätzen zu können.

Achtung

Natürlich enthält jede Unit mehr Aufgaben als eine normale Englischarbeit. Es ist also normal, dass Ihr Kind für die Bearbeitung einer Unit im Klassenarbeitstrainer länger braucht als für eine normale Arbeit.

Wir wünschen viel Spaß beim Lernen und eine erfolgreiche Klassenarbeit.
All the best

So bereitest du dich auf eine Arbeit vor

Damit du dich optimal auf eine Klassenarbeit vorbereiten kannst, musst du lernen, wie du richtig lernst. Das richtige Lernen bzw. Üben wird nicht von der Zahl der bearbeiteten Aufgaben, sondern viel mehr von der Lernatmosphäre und der Strukturierung des Lernprozesses, beeinflusst.

Die Lernatmosphäre vorbereiten

Eine ruhige, druckfreie Lernatmosphäre ist wichtig. Beim Lernen handelt es sich um eine bewertungsfreie Situation, in der das Üben im Vordergrund stehen soll. Es sollte dir möglich sein, angst- bzw. sorgenfrei **Fehler** zu machen und **Fragen** zu stellen. Dies ist wichtig für deinen Lernfortschritt.

Pausen gehören zum Lernprozess, denn sie helfen eine kognitive Überforderung zu verhindern. Auf eine 45-minütige Übungseinheit kann z.B. eine fünf- bis zehnminütige (Bewegungs-)Pause folgen.

Lerninhalte für die Klassenarbeit

Für eine erfolgreiche Vorbereitung ist es wichtig, die **Lerninhalte der Klassenarbeit** zu kennen. Du solltest dich daher mindestens eine Woche vor der Klassenarbeit bei der Fachlehrkraft informieren. Wenn du schon früher mit der Vorbereitung beginnen willst, kannst du im Inhaltsverzeichnis des Schülerbuchs (S. 4-9) nachschauen. Es besitzt eine ausführliche Übersicht über die Kompetenzen und sprachlichen Mittel (*vocabulary* & *grammar*), die du in jeder Unit vermittelt bekommst.

Ergänzende Materialien

Neben dem Klassenarbeitstrainer solltest du ein separates **Lernheft** führen. Dort kannst du die Arbeitsergebnisse zu den Aufgaben festhalten und so jede Aufgabe mehrfach bearbeiten.

Manchmal ist es ebenfalls hilfreich **eine Lernpartnerin oder einen Lernpartner** in der Klasse zu suchen. Ihr könnt euch unterstützen und bei Fragen und Problemen gegenseitig helfen.

Um keine der relevanten Kompetenzen zu vergessen, solltest du einen **Lernplan** erstellen. In diesem kannst du festhalten, was, wann geübt werden soll. Du kannst auch zusätzliche Übungsmöglichkeiten oder hilfreiche Schulbuchseiten notieren. Das Abhaken geübter Kompetenzen gibt dir einen Überblick über den Lernprozess bis zur Klassenarbeit. So könnte ein ausgefüllter Lernplan für Unit 4 aussehen:

Kompetenz / I can...	Sprachliche Mittel	Materialien	Wann übe ich das?	Erledigt?	Noch mal üben?
... talk about celebrations	Voc celebration words	SB, p. 98–99 Vocabulary p. 221–222	Mo. 20.11.	✓	nein
... describe a special meal	Voc food and drink, a box / carton / jar ... of ...	SB, pp. 100–103 Wordbank, p. 191 Vocabulary, p. 222	Mo. 20.11.	✓	ja, am Do. 23.11.
... describe a special meal	G some, any, a little, a few	G SB, p. 101 Language file, p. 179 Erklärfilm in der Cornelsen Lernen App	Di. 21.11.	✓	nein

Lernplan

💡

Um dich gut auf die kommende Englischarbeit vorzubereiten, solltest du dich frühzeitig informieren, welche Themen in der Arbeit drankommen. Damit du nichts vergisst und auch genug Zeit hast, um zu lernen, solltest du dir einen Lernplan erstellen. Du kannst diesen Plan als Vorlage nutzen:

Lernplan von: _____

Datum der Klassenarbeit: _____

Unit 1 / 2 / 3 / 4 / 5

Kompetenz / I can…	Sprachliche Mittel	Materialien	Wann übe ich das? (Datum)	Erledigt? (✓)	Noch mal üben? (ja/nein)

Unit 1
Travel and holidays

1 LISTENING **Sharing holiday stories** _____ / 12   ▶ SB, pp. 12–13, p. 185

🔊 01

a) Read the task carefully. Then listen to the conversation between Maya and Seth and tick (✓) the right answer – a) or b). One of the questions has two right answers.

Lies die Aufgabe sorgfältig durch. Höre dann das Gespräch zwischen Maya and Seth an und kreuze die richtige Antwort – a) oder b) – an. Eine der Fragen hat zwei richtige Antworten. (6 Punkte)

Maya ...

1 travelled to ...

   ☐ a) Italy.   ☐ b) Portugal.

2 stayed at ...

   ☐ a) a campsite.   ☐ b) grandma's house.

3 thought it was sometimes too ...

   ☐ a) sunny.   ☐ b) rainy.

Seth ...

4 travelled to ...

   ☐ a) Scotland.   ☐ b) Australia.

5 stayed at ...

   ☐ a) a campsite.   ☐ b) a hotel.

6 thought it was sometimes too ...

   ☐ a) cloudy.   ☐ b) rainy.

b) Read the sentences below. Listen again. True or false? Tick (✓).

Lies die untenstehenden Sätze. Höre noch einmal zu. Richtig oder falsch? Hake ab (✓). (6 Punkte)

		true	false
1	Maya was on holiday with her mum and dad.		
2	Summers are always very hot where Maya's grandma lives.		
3	There were sunny and rainy days when Seth was at the campsite.		
4	In Edinburgh, Seth's sister was tired.		
5	Maya was in Edinburgh this summer too.		
6	For Seth the festival wasn't very interesting.		

▶ Check ↵

2 READING **My Greek holiday** _____ / 5

▶ SB, pp. 15–16

Read Ella's travel blog. *Lies Ellas Reiseblog.*

Lies dir vor dem Lesen des Textes die Aufgabe zum Text gut durch und achte auf Schlüsselwörter. So weißt du, worauf du beim Lesen achten musst.

www.ellas-travelblog.example.net

Friday, July 21

Hi guys! It's Day 4 of our holiday in Greece. We're in Thessaloniki. We travelled here yesterday from Athens, first by train, then by plane. But the journey didn't start very well. After breakfast we walked to the train station. But we went the wrong way and got to the station late. We were lucky that the train was late too!

We flew to Thessaloniki on a small plane. I don't know why. Thessaloniki is not a small place. The journey was a little scary because the plane was so small and loud. My little brother Benji and I were happy when we arrived an hour later and got off the plane.

It's exciting to see the sights in Thessaloniki. Today we did a boat trip. It was a big boat with a cafe, a restaurant and four floors. It was so cool! The trip took four hours. I took a lot of photos of the sea and us. Then we had lunch in the restaurant and after that we played card games. Later Benji got up and walked away. When we didn't see him for 20 minutes, Dad and I started to worry about him. Mum was calm. "I'm sure he's OK," she said. Dad and I went to look for him. We found him in the kid's play area. He wasn't happy to see us. Dad said, "Come on, let's get some ice cream!" and Benji's eyes got big. Dad knows how to make us happy. 🙂

Bye for now,

Ella

Leave a comment

Circle the correct ending to complete the sentences.
Umkreise das korrekte Ende, um die Sätze zu vervollständigen.

1 Ella and her family travelled to Thessaloniki from Athens by plane. / train. / train and plane.

2 They got to the station late because they went the wrong way. / were slow. / woke up late.

3 Today they saw the sights and went to a cafe. / on a boat trip. / on a cool bike ride.

4 They were worried about Benji, so they went to get help. / get ice cream. / look for him.

5 Ella and her family were on the trip for four hours. / five hours. / six hours.

▶ Check

3 WORDS **Travel experiences** _____ / 7

► SB, pp. 14–16, pp. 24–25

Complete these comments on Ella's blog with the adjectives in the box.

Vervollständige diese Kommentare auf Ellas Blog mit den Adjektiven im Kasten.

angry • calm • easy • exciting • free • proud • scared

1 I really enjoyed your blog, Ella! I'm Greek and I'm so _____ of our wonderful country.

2 Boats are cool. They can be big, small, fast or slow. The journey is always _____!

3 I was on a boat in bad weather and it wasn't fun but I learned to be _____.

4 There's a cute little boat near my home that we can use for _____. I love going on it.

5 We took our dog Waldo on a boat ride and he was really scared. Then some people were

_____ at us because he barked so much. It wasn't an _____

journey.

6 My sister is _____ of travelling by plane. She doesn't like flying.

4 WORDS **A crossword** _____ / 10

► SB, p. 19, pp. 202–208

Read and look at the clues. Complete the crossword with the correct words.

Lies und schaue die Hinweise an. Vervollständige das Kreuzworträtsel mit den richtigen Wörtern.

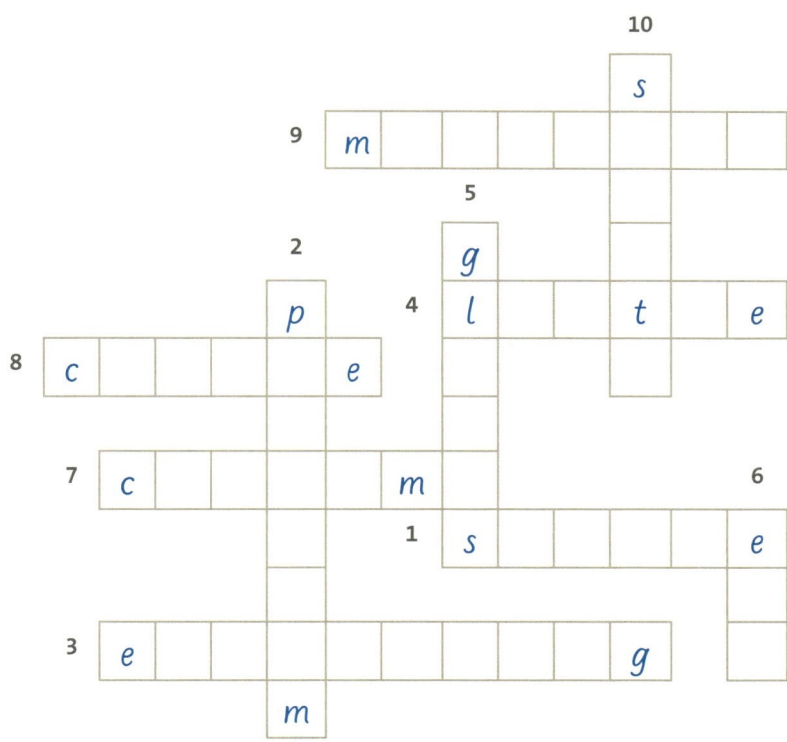

1 With this ticket you can travel in one direction.

2 It's where people stand to get on a train.

3 It's a word that means *all*.

4 It's another word for *small*.

5

6 You do it with food.

7 It's what you wear to a Halloween party.

8

9 A person who plays music.

10 Tourists like to see these.

► Check

Erklär-film

5 LANGUAGE **Sadie's day** _____ / 12

► SB, pp. 14–15, p. 171

Complete Sadie's journal entry with the verbs from the box. Use the correct positive forms of the simple past. *Vervollständige Sadies Tagebucheintrag mit den Verben aus dem Kasten. Benutze die korrekten positiven Formen des simple past.*

> be (2x) • eat • get up • have • help • like
> • listen • play • take • try • win

Saturday, 13th July

What an exciting day! I (1) _____ early because my team (2) _____

a game at 9:30 a.m. It (3) _____ the first game of the summer season and we

(4) _____ ! We (5) _____ really well. There (6) _____

lots of people there to watch us too. After the game Mum and Dad and I (7) _____

lunch at my favourite burger place. I (8) _____ a veggie burger for the first time and I

really (9) _____ it! Later I (10) _____ Dad with the food shopping. We

(11) _____ to my favourite music in the car. That was fun! In the evening after dinner I

(12) _____ the bus to Highgate Cinema to meet Ethan and see a scary vampire film.

Erklär-film

6 LANGUAGE **A great summer** _____ / 5

► SB, p. 20, p. 172

Alex had a boring summer, but he doesn't want his classmates to know that. Use the negative form and say how his summer really was. *Alex hatte einen langweiligen Sommer, aber er will nicht, dass seine Klassenkameraden das wissen. Benutze die Verneinung und sage, wie sein Sommer wirklich war.*

> Wenn du sagen willst, dass etwas nicht geschehen ist, setzt du *didn't* vor das Verb.
> Das Verb steht dann immer im Infinitiv (der Grundform): *She didn't finish.*

What Alex says	The real story
1 I went windsurfing every day.	*He didn't* _____ _____
2 My parents took me to Hollywood and I met Taylor Swift!	*His parents didn't* _____ _____
3 I learned to fly a plane.	*He didn't* _____ _____
4 I travelled all around England.	*He didn't* _____ _____
5 The zoo gave me a summer job working with the monkeys.	*The zoo didn't* _____ _____

► Check

7 MEDIATION **Night tour** _____ / 6 ▶ SB, p. 16, p. 164

You are on holiday in Northern England and your parents want to visit a castle. They see this information in a travel brochure and ask you to help them understand it. Look at the information, then answer your parents' questions. *Du bist im Urlaub in Nordengland und deine Eltern wollen ein Schloss besuchen. Sie sehen diese Informationen in einer Reisebroschüre und sie bitten dich, ihnen zu helfen, sie zu verstehen. Schaue dir die Informationen an und beantworte ihre Fragen.*

Experience Chillingham Castle

A long history
Chillingham Castle in Northumberland welcomes you!
Enjoy its stone towers, wonderful gardens, lakes
and parks. Learn about the long and often horrible
history of this great castle on our guided Castle Tour.

Night Tour
At night Chillingham doesn't sleep. Many visitors
see scary things in the castle halls. Come and experience
the castle on our special Night Tour.

Opening times
1st April – 5th November
11 am – 5 pm every day

Night Tour
For times and dates, see our website.
Night Tour ticket price £25.00

Ticket prices*
Adults   £11.00
Children (under 16)   £7.00
Family   £30.00 (2 adults + up to 3 children)

* Prices can change. Please check our website.

1 Was kann man um das Schloss herum sehen?

_____

2 Was steht da über die Geschichte des Schlosses?

_____

3 „Night Tour" verstehe ich schon. Aber was erlebt man dabei?

_____

4 Wie sind die Öffnungszeiten für das Schloss?

_____

5 Was ist günstiger für uns drei – eine Familienkarte oder drei individuelle Karten?

_____

6 Irgendwie reizt mich diese Night Tour. Wann findet sie statt?

_____

▶ Check ↴

8 WRITING Gita and Arun in Edinburgh _____ / 15   ▶ More help, p. 75 ▶ SB, pp. 28–29

Look at the pictures. Then write the story about this sister and brother on their family holiday. Write about 80 words or more. Use the simple past. The words in the box can help you. *Schaue die Bilder an. Schreibe dann die Geschichte über den Familienurlaub dieser Geschwister. Schreibe etwa 80 Wörter oder mehr. Benutze das simple past. Die Wörter im Kasten können dir helfen.*

> to arrive • to get off • to stay • to shop • to watch • busy • cheap • cool • excited • exciting • free •
> fun • clothes • costume • mask • (street) musician • vampire

Their train arrived at the station in Edinburgh and Gita and Arun _____

_____

At McPurdy's Hostel _____

_____

Later the family went for a walk in the city and _____

_____

_____

_____

That evening, Gita and Arun _____

_____

▶ Check

9 STUDY SKILLS **Lost and found** _____ / 6　　　　► SB, p. 28

Linking words can help make a story interesting. Use _or_, _and_ or _but_ to link the two sentences together.
Verbindungswörter können dazu beitragen, eine Geschichte interessant zu machen. Benutze or, and, _oder_ but, _um die beiden Sätze zu verbinden._

1　It was nearly dark. Their destination was more than a kilometre away.

　　It was nearly dark and their destination was more than a kilometre away.

2　She guided the group of kids through the fields. She didn't know the way.

　　_____

3　"Do we turn left at the next road? Do we turn right?"

　　_____

4　Her phone was dead. The little kids in the group didn't have phones.

　　_____

5　"We can stop here and wait for help. We can try to find the way back."

　　_____

6　She hoped for a light or a sound. That's when she heard the noise.

　　_____

7　She wasn't sure what it was. She knew it came from the campsite.

　　_____

Bereich	Aufgabe	erreichte Punktzahl	🤩	😎	🤔	😭
listening	1	_____ / 12	12–11	10–9	8–6	5–0
reading	2	_____ / 5	5	4	3	2–0
words	3	_____ / 7 ⎫ _____ /17	17–16	15–12	11–9	8–0
	4	_____ / 10 ⎭				
language	5	_____ / 12 ⎫ _____ /17	17–16	15–12	11–9	8–0
	6	_____ / 5 ⎭				
mediation	7	_____ / 6	6	5	4–3	2–0
writing	8	_____ / 15	15–14	13–11	10–8	7–0
skills	9	_____ / 6	6	5	4–3	2–0
Gesamt		_____ / 78	78–71	70–55	54–39	38–0

Unit 2
Friends and heroes

1 LISTENING **Interesting people** _____ / 12   ▸ SB, pp. 40–43, p. 186

🔊 02

a) Look at the pictures. How do the four kids look? Listen to the conversation between Ruby and Ellis and match the names with the pictures. _Schaue die Bilder an. Wie sehen die vier Kinder aus? Höre dem Gespräch zwischen Ruby und Ellis zu und verbinde die Namen mit den Bildern. (4 Punkte)_

| Kisi | Jayden | Luis | Vera |

b) Read the sentences. Listen again and complete them with the correct words from the box.
Lies die Sätze. Höre noch einmal zu und vervollständige sie mit den korrekten Wörter aus dem Kasten.
(8 Punkte)

activist • basketball • confident • helpful • jokes • next to • quiet • try

1 Kisi sits _____ Ruby in English.

2 She tells really funny _____.

3 Luis doesn't _____ to be funny, but Ellis laughs a lot when he's around.

4 He's good at sports and plays on the _____ team.

5 Jayden was very _____ when Ellis tried to talk to him in the canteen.

6 Ruby likes that Jayden is always _____ when she has computer problems.

7 Vera is very strong and _____.

8 Vera wants to become an _____ when she gets older.

▸ Check ⤴

2 READING **A normal hero** _____ / 6

▶ SB, pp. 46–49

Read the text and the sentences below. True or false? Tick (✓).
Lies den Text und die Sätze unten. Richtig oder falsch? Markiere (✓).

On a cloudy Saturday afternoon Lyle and Bashir sat in the cinema at Churchill Square. They ate popcorn and watched the teen superheroes Zap and Astrogirl. Zap wore a blue cape and a silver mask with a robot eye. Astrogirl had purple hair and wore a black cape and high boots. The pair were funny and confident. They used their superpowers to fight some horrible monsters and, in the end, save New York City.

Outside, after the film, Lyle and Bashir stood with their bikes, ready to ride home.

"Those guys were amazing," Lyle said.

"Yes, they were. It's a shame that we don't know any superheroes," Bashir said.

"That's true," Lyle said. He felt very normal, but he dreamed of being a hero.

A moment later Lyle saw a man running with a rucksack in his hand. Lyle tried to move, but the man ran into Lyle's bike and fell to the ground. His rucksack flew from his hand.

"Ahh! My leg!" he said. He tried to stand up. "Where's my rucksack?!" he said.

Lyle felt bad. "Wait! You're hurt. Let me help you," he said. Lyle took out his phone and called 999. The man looked worried. Lyle tried to help him stay calm. Soon the police[1] and an ambulance arrived. People watched and some took photos. The police wrote down Lyle's name and address.

Then they took the man to the hospital.

"I hope I'm not in trouble," Lyle said to Bashir.

The next morning Lyle came into the kitchen.

"That was very brave, Lyle," his mum said.

"Yes. We read what happened," his dad said.

Lyle was surprised. He saw the newspaper on the table. On the front page it said, "BOY STOPS DANGEROUS THIEF[2]". There was a photo of Lyle with the man on the ground. The article said the man tried to run from police after he took a lot of money in a rucksack. A brave teenager, Lyle B., stopped the man, stayed with him and called the police.

Lyle didn't understand. _Dangerous? Thief?_

"You're a hero, Lyle," his mum said. "We're so proud of you. How do you feel?"

Lyle didn't feel like a hero. "I'm hungry. What's for breakfast?"

[1] **police** _die Polizei_   [2] **thief** _Dieb_

		true	false
1	After the film, Lyle wanted to be a hero like Zap and Astrogirl.		
2	The man fell because Lyle's bike was in his way.		
3	Lyle called 999 because he wanted to help the man.		
4	The police told Lyle that he was in trouble.		
5	Lyle's parents found out what happened when they read the newspaper.		
6	Lyle knew that he was a superhero, but he didn't want to tell his parents.		

▶ Check

3 WORDS **Parts of the body**   _____ / 10

▶ SB, p. 188

Look at Astrogirl. Write the names of the parts of the body on the numbered lines. The first letter is already there. *Schaue Astrogirl an. Schreibe die Namen der Körperteile auf die nummerierten Linien. Der erste Buchstabe ist schon vorhanden.*

1 *e* _____

2 *n* _____

3 *h* _____

4 *e* _____

5 *f* _____

6 *a* _____

7 *h* _____

8 *l* _____

9 *a* _____

10 *f* _____

4 WORDS **Describing people and things**   _____ / 7

▶ SB, p. 48, p. 157

Complete the statements with the correct word from the box. There is one word too many in the box. *Vervollständige die Aussagen mit dem korrekten Wort aus dem Kasten. Es gibt ein Wort zu viel im Kasten.*

confident • dangerous • honest • kind • tidy • unfair • unhappy • untidy

1 Our parents taught us to be _____ to people. Always help when

you can.

2 Look at his room – dirty clothes are everywhere! My room is never _____

like this.

3 He gave her a sweet but he didn't give me one. It was so _____!

4 Erin was really _____ after she and her football team lost the big

game.

5 That was a great presentation. You looked very _____.

6 To be _____, I can't say what the book is about. I didn't read it.

7 Cycling can be _____ if you don't wear a helmet.

▶ Check

5 LANGUAGE **Meeting a sports hero** _____ / 10

▶ SB, pp. 46–47, p. 175

Katie Dixon, 23, is an Olympic swimmer from Brighton. Her old school invited her for a visit. *Katie Dixon, 23, ist eine olympische Schwimmerin aus Brighton. Ihre alte Schule hat sie zu einem Besuch eingeladen.*

a) Write the students' questions in the simple past. Then write Katie's short answers. *Schreibe die Fragen der Schülerinnen und Schüler im simple past. Dann schreibe Katies Kurzantworten. (6 Punkte)*

1 _____ (you, go) to this school – really? Yes, <u>I did</u>. Just like you.

2 _____ (you, wear) a blue uniform too? No, <u>I didn't</u>. Mine was red.

3 _____ (the school, have)
a canteen when you were a student? Yes, <u>it did</u>. I ate there a lot.

4 <u>Did you walk</u> to school? No, _____. I came by bus.

5 <u>Did you get</u> lots of homework? Yes, _____. I didn't like that.

6 <u>Did your parents make</u> you swim? No, _____. I wanted to do it.

> **!**
>
> Fragen im *simple past* bildest du mit *did* und dem Infinitiv des Verbs: *Did you like this school?*
> Kurzantworten bildest du mit *did* oder *didn't*: *Yes, I did. / No, I didn't.*
> Auch bei Fragen mit Fragewörtern verwendest du bei allen Personen *did* und das Verb im Infinitiv:
> *When did you go to this school?*

Erklär-film

b) The students had more questions for Katie. Complete the questions in the simple past with the right question word from the box. *Die Schülerinnen und Schüler hatten noch mehr Fragen an Katie. Vervollständige die Fragen mit dem simple past und mit dem richtigen Fragewort aus dem Kasten. (4 Punkte)*

how • what • when • why

1 _____ (you, learn) to swim? I learned when I was four.

2 _____ (you, become) a swimmer? Because I love swimming. That's all.

3 _____ (you, get ready) for the Olympics? I swam a lot and ate well.

4 _____ (you, do) before each race? I listened to quiet music.

▶ Check 🔖

6 MEDIATION Eine Klassenfahrt _____ / 6   ▶ SB, pp. 52–53, pp. 164–165

Neve, an Irish exchange student in your class, sees this article in the online student newspaper and asks you to help her understand it. Read the article and answer her questions. *Neve, eine irische Austauschschülerin in deiner Klasse, sieht diesen Artikel in der Online-Schülerzeitung und bittet dich, ihr zu helfen, ihn zu verstehen. Lies den Artikel und beantworte ihre Fragen.*

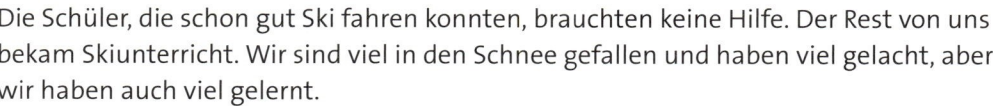

www.schillerschulenews.example.net

Unsere Schule   Unsere Stadt   Sport   AGs   Musik und Film   Leserbriefe   Comics

Eine Klassenfahrt in die Berge *von Linus Kramer*

Letzte Woche hat unsere Klasse – die 9B – einen viertägigen Skiausflug gemacht. Das war aufregend! Die Fahrt mit dem Bus dauerte fünf Stunden. Unser Busfahrer war ein cooler Typ mit langen Haaren und Sonnenbrille. Er war auch witzig. Ein paar Mal hat er Witze erzählt und alle zum Lachen gebracht.

Als wir am Hotel ankamen, lag jede Menge Schnee. Es war sonnig und perfekt zum Skifahren!

Am nächsten Morgen bekamen wir unsere Ausrüstung. Die Schüler, die schon gut Ski fahren konnten, brauchten keine Hilfe. Der Rest von uns bekam Skiunterricht. Wir sind viel in den Schnee gefallen und haben viel gelacht, aber wir haben auch viel gelernt.

Leider gab es ein paar Unfälle. Lea ist gestürzt und hat sich den Knöchel verletzt. Und Jonas fuhr einmal zu schnell den Berg hinunter, und krachte in Yusuf hinein. Yusuf verletzte sich am Bein und konnte für den Rest des Tages nicht mehr Ski fahren. Unsere beiden Lehrer, Frau Ramos und Herr Gorek, waren sehr besorgt und hätten beinahe einen Krankenwagen gerufen. Danach haben wir ihnen alle versprochen vorsichtiger zu sein.

1 Neve: I know that "Klassenfahrt" means class trip. How long were they away?

You: _____

2 Neve: Is he saying that the bus driver was "cool"? Why?

You: _____

3 Neve: What was the weather like when they arrived?

You: _____

4 Neve: Did some students get ski lessons? Was it hard for them to learn?

You: _____

5 Neve: Hey, I know Lea! What does he say about her?

You: _____

6 Neve: And what happened to Yusuf? I see his name two times.

You: _____

▶ Check 🔁

7 WRITING **One of my friends** _____ / 15

▶ More Help, pp. 76 ▶ SB, pp. 40–43, p. 186

Look at the online post about someone's friend. Write a post about one of your friends. *Schaue den Post über eine Freundin von jemandem an. Schreibe einen Beitrag über eine Freundin oder einen Freund von dir.*

Write about:
– what he/she is like (looks, personality)
– how you met
– why you are happy to be friends with this person

Use the words in the box or your own. Write 60 words or more.

Schreibe über:
– *was für ein Typ er/sie ist (Aussehen, Persönlichkeit)*
– *wir ihr euch kennengelernt habt*
– *warum du froh bist, mit dieser Person befreundet zu sein*

Du kannst die Wörter im Kasten verwenden oder deine eigene. Schreibe 60 Wörter oder mehr.

evie_sundowner43

evie_sundowner43 Ginny and I met at music school last year. She's so cool and she always listens to my ideas. We often write songs …

black • blond • blue • braces • brown • dark • curly • eyes • glasses • hair • long • red • short • straight
brave • clever • confident • cool • fair • friendly • funny • good at/with … • helpful • honest • kind • polite • quiet • nice
The first time we met was … • I think we met at/when … • We became friends when/after/ …
I like her/him because … • She/He's a great friend because … • When I'm with her/him, …

_____

_____

_____

_____

_____

_____

_____

_____

_____

▶ Check

Erklär-film

8 SMALL CAPS: STUDY SKILLS **Finding the right words** _____ / 7   ► SB, p. 56, p. 158

Read the sentences. Use a word from the same word family as the word in brackets to complete each sentence. *Lies die Sätze. Benutze ein Wort aus der gleichen Wortfamilie wie das Wort in Klammern, um jeden Satz zu vervollständigen.*

> Ein Wort gehört immer zu einer Wortfamilie. Kennst du ein Wort aus der Wortfamilie, z.B. das Verb *(to) act*, verstehst du auch die Nomen *action* und *activity* und das Adjektiv *active*. Mit den Regeln zur Wortbildung kannst du die Bedeutung ableiten.

1   I'm planning a big birthday party. Did you get my _____? (invite)

2   She's such an amazing _____. Look how fast she goes up the wall! (climb)

3   It's nice to have friendly _____ who are always ready to help. (neighbourhood)

4   Her train is still not here! Did we read the _____ time right? (arrive)

5   Thank you for driving us to the station.

   That is very _____. (help)

6   He was _____ for two weeks.

   Today is his first day back at school. (illness)

7   I don't like vampire films.

   They're too _____ for me. (scare)

Bereich	Aufgabe	erreichte Punktzahl	🤩	😎	🥺	😭
listening	1	_____ / 12	12–11	10–8	7–6	5–0
reading	2	_____ / 6	6	5–4	3	2–0
words	3	_____ / 10 ⎫ _____ /17	17–15	14–12	11–9	8–0
	4	_____ / 7 ⎭				
language	5	_____ / 10	10–9	8–7	6–5	4–0
mediation	6	_____ / 6	6	5–4	3	2–0
writing	7	_____ / 15	15–14	13–11	10–8	7–0
skills	8	_____ / 7	7	6–5	5–4	3–0
Gesamt		_____ / 73	73–66	65–51	50–37	36–0

► Check ⤵

Unit 3
Activities and games

1 LISTENING **Planning a visit** _____ / 11

03

a) **Yusuf's cousin Selma is going to visit him in Brighton next weekend. They're making plans on the phone. Listen to their conversation and tick (✓) the five correct activities they choose. There is one extra picture.** _Yusufs Cousine Selma wird ihn nächstes Wochenende in Brighton besuchen. Sie machen Pläne am Telefon. Höre ihrem Gespräch zu and hake (✓) die fünf korrekten Aktivitäten ab, die sie auswählen. Es gibt ein zusätzliches Bild. (5 Punkte)_

A

B

C

D

E

F

💡 Mache dir kurze Notizen auf einem Notizzettel oder mit Bleistift auf deinem Aufgabenblatt. Bleibe ruhig, wenn du beim ersten Mal nicht alles verstehst. Du hörst den Text meist zweimal.

b) **Read the sentences below. Listen again. True or false? Tick the correct answer (✓).** _Lies die Sätze unten. Höre dann noch einmal zu. Richtig oder falsch? Hake ab (✓). (6 Punkte)_

		true	false
1	Selma's last visit to Brighton was last summer.		
2	Selma is going to arrive in Brighton on Friday at 7 in the evening.		
3	Yusuf's mum is going to make chicken curry for dinner.		
4	The zip wire at Brighton Beach is more exciting than the i360 tower.		
5	Yusuf knows a place where they can eat lunch.		
6	Selma wants to do something in the afternoon that's free.		

► Check ⬐

3

2 READING **Film reviews** _____ / 7

►SB, pp. 76–78, p. 189

It's Saturday evening and Selma and Yusuf want to watch a film online. Read the film reviews.
Es ist Samstag Abend und Selma und Yusuf wollen einen Film online schauen. Lies die Rezensionen.

Never Stop

Hold on to your seat as three friends go on the adventure of their lives in *Never Stop*. Jenna Colman plays the energetic and sporty Lottie, who finds out that a classmate, Bren, is in trouble. Lottie and her friends Alma and Doro are ready to help. They must find Bren, but East London is a big, dangerous place.
Rating: ★ ★ ★

The Superlatives – Home Sweet Home

The Superlatives, your favourite cartoon superhero family, is back again! Flashman, Supernova, Pixie Pop and Airdot are just trying to save the world. It's their job! But life's other challenges, like homework, dating, bad hair and tidying the kitchen, are alwyays getting in the way. *The Superlatives – Home Sweet Home* is the funniest superhero film ever.
Rating: ★ ★ ★ ★ ★

Play for your life

In *Play for your life* Kid Walker lives inside a video game where he and his friend Amelia must find their way through dangerous worlds – dark forests, underwater cities and far-away planets. With each click and each new world, Kid faces new dangers. Amazing special effects, weird characters and a clever story make *Play for your life* one of the best sci-fi films of the year.
Rating: ★ ★ ★ ★

Read the reviews and complete the sentences.
Lies die Rezensionen und vervollständige die Sätze.

1 The main character in *Never Stop* is _____ .

2 *Never Stop* takes place in _____ .

3 The Superlatives are a _____ family.

4 If you like funny films, _____ is the best film to see.

5 *Play for your life* is one of the best sci-fi films of the year because it has amazing special

_____ , weird _____ and a _____ story.

6 The film with the best rating is _____ .

7 The film with the worst rating is _____ .

 ►Check

3 WORDS **An amazing evening** _____ / 6 ▶ SB, pp. 216–221

Beth is writing about a special summer event for her school's online newspaper. Some words are mixed up. Complete the sentences with the correct word. _Beth schreibt über ein besonderes Sommerereignis für die Online-Schülerzeitschrift ihrer Schule. Einige Worte sind durcheinander. Vervollständige ihre Sätze mit dem korrekten Wort._

Something special is happening at the Brighton Pavilion.

If you love music, street dance and

(1) _____ (EAEHTTR), then don't miss

Streetbeats. It's more than a musical. The sounds, colours

and costumes are so (2) _____ (ACREVIET),

they're like nothing else that I know. And the dancing is

fast and (3) _____ (ERENGECIT). Alma Luna and Joe Cooper are the two

(4) _____ (TARSITS) who (5) _____ (EARTCED) _Streetbeats_.

Their first show three years ago wasn't as exciting as this one. It's clear that Alma, Joe and their group

(6) _____ (ERPARPDE) a lot for this show. _Streetbeats_ is only playing for two more

weeks, so get your tickets now.

4 WORDS **Music, films and shows** _____ / 8 ▶ SB, pp. 78–79, pp. 217–218

Match the descriptions with the correct word. _Verbinde die Beschreibungen mit dem korrekten Wort._

1 This is what you watch to find out what a film is like.

2 These are people who watch a film or show.

3 In this kind of film or show, people sing a lot.

4 Without these, action films can be boring.

5 These are the words of a song.

6 This describes something that is not good at all.

7 This is where a story finishes.

8 This is a person in a film or a story.

A musical

B terrible

C character

D trailer

E ending

F audience

G special effects

H lyrics

▶ Check

3

5 WORDS Finding Amelia _____ / 7

▶ SB, pp. 80–81, p. 90, pp. 218–219

In the video game version of Play for your life, Kid Walker must follow directions to find his friend Amelia. Match the directions and the pictures. *In der Videospiel-Version von Play for your life, muss Kid Walker den Wegbeschreibungen folgen, um seine Freundin Amelia zu finden. Ordne die Wegbeschreibungen den richtigen Bildern zu.*

1 Go across the bridge.
2 Turn left at the wall.
3 Go straight on.
4 Go up the stairs.

5 Turn right.
6 Go through the forest.
7 Go past the big tree.
8 Go down the hill.

1	2	3	4
5	**6**	**7**	**8**
A			

6 LANGUAGE What do you think? _____ / 8

▶ SB, pp. 76–78, p. 178

Erklär-film

Complete the sentences with the comparative and the superlative form of the adjective in brackets. *Vervollständige die Sätze mit der komparativen Form und der superlativen Form des Adjektivs in Klammern.*

1 I think that pop music is *louder than* acoustic music. But rock music is the *loudest*. (loud)

2 I think that thrillers are _____ action films. But sci-fi films are

_____. (exciting)

3 I think cartoons are _____ game shows. But comedies are

_____. (funny)

4 I think sushi is _____ pizza. But fish and chips are

_____. (good)

5 I think musicians are _____ footballers. But actors are

_____. (cool)

▶ Check

7 LANGUAGE **Activity week** _____ / 10   ▸ SB, pp. 72–75, pp. 176–177

Longhill High School is having an assembly. The head teacher, Mrs Harrison, is talking to students about next week's Activity Week. *Die Longhill High School hält eine Versammlung. Die Schulleiterin, Frau Harrison, redet mit den Schülern und Schülerinnen über die Activity Week, die nächste Woche ist.*

> **!**
> Mit *going to* … sagst du, was du vorhast oder planst. *I'm going to make a cake.*
> *Going to* hat hier nichts mit dem deutschen „gehen" zu tun, sondern bedeutet „werden."

a) **Complete Mrs Harrison's statements with the correct form of the going to-future.** *Vervollständige die Aussagen von Frau Harrison mit der korrekten Form des going to-future. (6 Punkte)*

1 Next week we _____ (have)

Activity Week at our school.

2 It _____ (not, be) like last year,

when we only had activities on some days.

3 You _____ (do) different

activities every day.

4 You _____ (not, have) classes in

the afternoon.

5 Two popular rappers _____ (teach) you how to make rap music.

6 And Mr Shaw, a professional football trainer, _____ (explain) why

teamwork is important in sports and in life.

b) **Complete the students' questions to Mrs Harrison and her short answers. Use the correct form of the going to-future.** *Vervollständige die Fragen der Schüler und Schülerinnen an Frau Harrison und ihre Kurzantworten. Benutze die korrekte Form des going to-future. (4 Punkte)*

1 Question: _____ (we / do) activities all week?

Answer: Yes, _____.

2 Q: _____ (you / open) the canteen for snacks?

A: No, _____. But you can bring healthy snacks from home, if you'd like.

3 Q: When _____ (Mr Shaw / give) his talk?

A: At 2 p.m. on Monday.

4 Q: How _____ (we / get) the schedule of activities every day?

A: I'm going to ask your teacher to put the schedule on the board in your classroom.

▸ Check 🔖

8 MEDIATION A noisy cafe _____ / 6

► SB, pp. 76–77, p. 164

You're visiting London with your parents. You're sharing a table in a busy cafe with a chatty English woman. The cafe is noisy and your parents can't understand everything, so you help them. *Du besuchst London mit deinen Eltern. Ihr teilt euch einen Tisch in einem hektischen Café mit einer gesprächigen englischen Frau. Das Café ist laut und deine Eltern können nicht alles verstehen, also du hilfst ihnen.*

Woman: Are the cafes in Germany as noisy as this one?

Mum: Was hat sie gesagt?

You: Sie fragt, ob die Cafés in Deutschland so laut wie dieses Café sind.

Mum: Sag ihr bitte, dass sie noch lauter sind.

Dad: Ach nein, sie sind nicht so laut wie hier.

You: My mum says (1) _____

_____ , but my dad says

(2) _____

Woman: Oh, how funny! So are you enjoying London?

Mum: Sind wir was?

You: Sie will wissen, ob ihr London genießt.

Mum: Oh, yes! Erm, ich finde es sehr spannend.

Dad: Ach. Ich denke, es ist zu hektisch. Zu viele Autos und Busse und zu viele Menschen.

You: My mum thinks (3) _____

But my dad thinks (4) _____

Woman: I agree with your dad. Are you going to visit any museums?

Dad: Das habe ich nicht mitbekommen.

You: Sie stimmt dir zu, Papa. Werden wir noch irgendwelche Museen besuchen?

Mum: Yes, erm, morgen werden wir zum British Museum gehen. Aber heute Nachmittag werden wir noch mit dem Bus zu Covent Garden fahren. Bitte sag ihr das, Schatz.

You: Yes, tomorrow (5) _____

But this afternoon (6) _____

Woman: Covent Garden? That sounds great! Have fun!

► Check

9 WRITING **It's going to be cool!** _____ / 15

▶ More help, p. 77 ▶ SB, pp. 72–73

You're texting with a classmate who wasn't at the school assembly today. Look at the timetable and answer her questions about Sports Week. Name at least three activities that you're going to do. For each activity think about what, when and where. _Du schreibst eine SMS an eine Schulkameradin, die heute nicht bei der Schulversammlung war. Schaue den Zeitplan an und beantworte ihre Fragen zur Sports Week. Nenne mindestens drei Aktivitäten, die du tun wirst. Für jede Aktivität denke an was, wann und wo._

	ASSEMBLY HALL	GYM	SPORTS FIELD
SPORTS WEEK			
MON	12:45 Sports Week assembly	1:00 Fun with gymnastics 2:30 Gymnastics level 1	1:00 Football level 1 2:30 Golf level 1
TUES	12:45 Table tennis level 1 2:15 Table tennis level 2	12:45 Basketball level 1 2:15 Volleyball level 1	12:45 Cricket level 1 2:15 Tennis level 1
WED	12:45 Judo level 1 2:15 Judo level 2	12:45 Volleyball level 2 2:15 Gymnastics level 2	12:45 Football level 2 2:15 Tennis level 2
THURS	12:45 Boxing level 1 2:15 Boxing level 2	12:45 Basketball level 2 2:15 Gymnastics final	12:45 Cricket level 2 2:15 Cricket final
FRI	12:45 Table tennis final 2:15 Judo final	12:45 Basketball final 2:15 Volleyball final	12:45 Football final 2:15 Tennis final

Did they talk about Sports Week at the assembly today? What activities are you going to do? Hey, let's do an activity together! Maybe tennis, if it's in the timetable? ✓

on Monday/Tuesday /... • in the assembly hall / gym • at the sports field • at 12:45/2:15/...

Yes, they talked about Sports Week.

On Monday,

On Tuesday,

I like your idea! We can

▶ Check

10 STUDY SKILLS **That's my opinion** _____ / 6   ▶ SB, p. 86, p. 167

Complete the dialogue with the correct words and parts of phrases from the box. There is one phrase you don't need. *Vervollständige die Dialoge mit den korrekten Wörtern und Satzteilen aus dem Kasten. Es gibt einen Satzteil, den du nicht brauchst.*

> I agree • I don't agree • my opinion • that isn't true •
> You're right. • think • do you think

Amal Why do people worry so much about screen time? In (1) _____, there's

nothing bad about spending four hours at a computer or tablet.

Sam Hm. For me (2) _____. Four hours at a screen is not good for your eyes.

Jess (3) _____ with Sam. I get a headache after just one hour on my phone.

Amal But Jess, the screen on your phone is much smaller. That's why you get a headache.

Jess (4) _____. It is smaller than a tablet or computer screen. But too much

time in front of any screen is just not healthy. What (5) _____, Danny?

Danny I (6) _____ maybe everybody is different. Maybe four hours of screen

time is fine for Amal but not fine for somebody else.

Sam That's not what I read online.

Amal Let's research this question. Then we can discuss it more.

Bereich	Aufgabe	erreichte Punktzahl		🤩	😎	🤔	😭
listening	1	_____ / 11		11–10	9–8	1–6	5–0
reading	2	_____ / 7		6	5	4–3	2–0
words	3	_____ / 6	_____ /21	21–19	18–15	14–11	10–0
	4	_____ / 8					
	5	_____ / 7					
language	6	_____ / 8	_____ /18	18–17	16–13	12–9	8–0
	7	_____ / 10					
mediation	8	_____ / 6		6	5	4–3	2–0
writing	9	_____ / 15		15–14	13–11	10–8	7–0
skills	10	_____ / 6		6	5	4–3	2–0
Gesamt		_____ / 84		84–76	75–59	58–42	41–0

▶ Check 🔖

BASIC

lighthouse 2

Klassenarbeitstrainer

Lösungen

Cornelsen

◀) **1** LISTENING **Sharing holiday stories**
01
Hörtext

Seth	How were your summer holidays, Maya?
Maya	Oh, really nice.
Seth	Where were you?
Maya	I was in Portugal with my mum and dad. We visited my grandma.
Seth	Oh, nice! What was the weather like?
Maya	It was sunny and really hot every day.
Seth	Wow. Are summers always like that in Portugal?
Maya	They're sunny and warm, but they're not always that hot. Not in my grandma's town.
Seth	Were you at the beach a lot?
Maya	Yeah. We were there often.
Seth	When we were in Croatia last summer it was really hot too. We ate a lot of watermelon and ice cream!
Maya	We were lucky because my grandma's house is nice and cool inside. I was almost never outside in the afternoon. It was too hot. That was boring sometimes. What about you, Seth? Where were you in the summer holidays?
Seth	I was in Scotland with my sister and my dad.
Maya	Ooh, I like Scotland. Were you in a holiday apartment?
Seth	No, first we were at a campsite in the country.
Maya	Cool! Was it nice?
Seth	For the first three days it was really nice. The weather was sunny and we were outside all day. But then it rained for two days. That wasn't much fun.
Maya	How long were you there?
Seth	We were at the campsite for eight days. Then we went to the Edinburgh Festival.
Maya	Edinburgh! We were there last summer! I loved it. What was it like for you?
Seth	We were there for two days. Lots of visitors were in the city for the festival. We stayed in a small hotel. My sister was tired and ready to go home, but for me it was exciting watching all the street musicians.
Maya	Wow. What a great holiday!

a)

Maya ...

1 travelled to ...

☐ a) Italy. ☑ b) Portugal.

 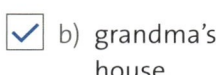

2 stayed at ...

☐ a) a campsite. ☑ b) grandma's house.

3 thought it was sometimes too ...

☑ a) sunny. ☐ b) rainy.

Seth ...

4 travelled to ...

☑ a) Scotland. ☐ b) Australia.

5 stayed at ...

☑ a) a campsite. ☑ b) a hotel.

6 thought it was sometimes too ...

☐ a) cloudy. ☑ b) rainy.

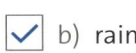 

b)

		true	false
1	Maya was on holiday with her mum and dad.	✓	
2	Summers are always very hot where Maya's grandma lives.		✓
3	There were sunny and rainy days when Seth was at the campsite.	✓	
4	In Edinburgh, Seth's sister was tired.	✓	
5	Maya was in Edinburgh this summer too.		✓
6	For Seth the festival wasn't very interesting.		✓

2 READING My Greek holiday

1 Ella and her family travelled to Thessaloniki from Athens by **train and plane**.
2 They got to the station late because they **went the wrong way**.
3 Today they saw the sights and went **on a boat trip**.
4 They were worried about Benji, so they went to **look for him**.
5 Ella and her family were on the trip for **four hours**.

Nutze unterschiedliche Möglichkeiten, um englische Texte zu hören. Wähle etwas aus, was dir gefällt, z.B. dein Lieblingslied oder dein Lieblingsbuch als Hörbuch auf Englisch. Schaue Filme und Serien auf Englisch. Blende Untertitel ein, falls du Probleme beim Verstehen hast. Blende sie aus, wenn du dich sicherer fühlst oder eine Episode schon mehrfach gesehen hast.

3 WORDS Travel experiences

1 proud · **2** exciting · **3** calm · **4** free · **5** angry; easy ·
6 scared

4 WORDS **A crossword**

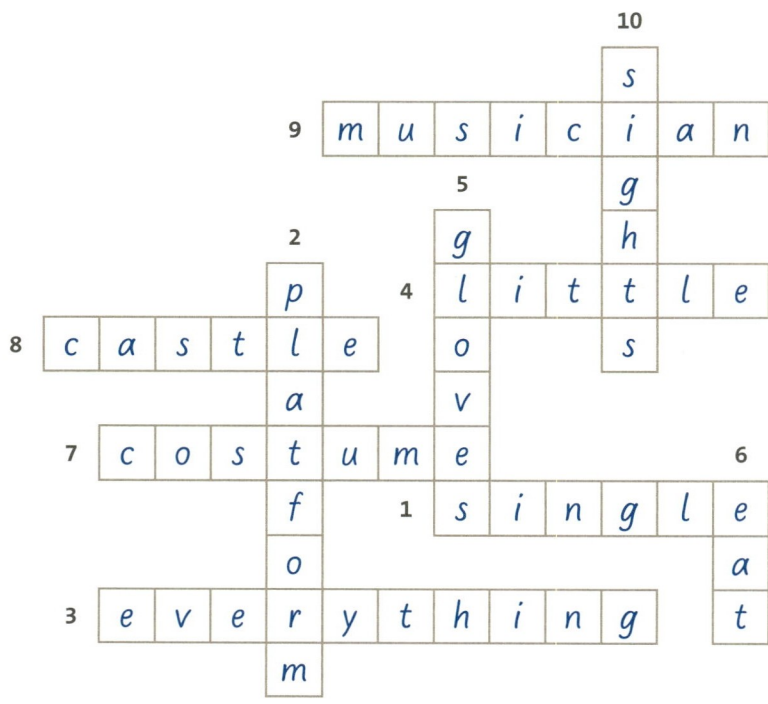

5 LANGUAGE **Sadie's day**

1 got up · **2** had · **3** was · **4** won · **5** played · **6** were · **7** ate · **8** tried · **9** liked · **10** helped ·
11 listened · **12** took

6 LANGUAGE **A great summer**

1   He didn't go windsurfing every day.
2   His parents didn't take to him Hollywood and he didn't meet Taylor Swift.
3   He didn't learn to fly a plane.
4   He didn't travel all around England.
5   The zoo didn't give him a summer job working with the monkeys.

> **!**
> Wenn Didi kommt,
> muss Ede gehen!

7 MEDIATION **Night tour**

1   Es gibt Gärten, einen See und eine große Parkanlage.
2   Es hat eine lange und oft grausame Geschichte. Geister sind auch Teil seiner Geschichte.
3   Man kann das Schloss am Abend besuchen und man kann schaurige Sachen erleben.
4   Es hat täglich von 11 bis 17 Uhr auf.
5   Zusammen gerechnet lohnt sich eine Familienkarte für uns nicht. Individuelle Karten sind insgesamt
    günstiger.
6   Man muss auf der Webseite schauen, wann die Touren stattfinden.

8 WRITING Gita and Arun in Edinburgh

Benutze die Checkliste um zu kontrollieren, ob du die Aufgabe erfüllt hast.

Does your text ...		
describe what happens in all the pictures?	*ja = 2 Punkte pro Bild* *zum Teil = 1 Punkt pro Bild*	
picture 1	train station • to arrive • to get off	_____ / 2
picture 2	hostel • cheap • stay • bed	_____ / 2
picture 3	to watch • street artist/musician • free • poster	_____ / 2
picture 4	clothes • cheap • to shop • costume	_____ / 2
picture 5	disco • theatre • costume	_____ / 2
picture 6	vampire • cool • exciting • mask	_____ / 2
have about 80 words?	*ja = 3 Punkte* *60–70 Wörter = 2 Punkte* *< 60 Wörter = 1 Punkt*	_____ / 3
	Total:	_____ / 15

(Lösungsbeispiel)

Their train arrived at the station in Edinburgh and Gita and Arun got off the train with their mum and dad. They walked to a cheap hostel near the station. At McPurdy's Hostel, Arun relaxed in his bed while his dad changed his clothes. Gita and her mum looked at some information about the Edinburgh Festival. Later the family walked around in the city and watched the street artists. Then Gita and Arun saw a poster for a free costume disco. They liked the idea. They went to a second-hand clothes shop and shopped for cheap clothes for costumes. That evening, Gita and Arun went to the costume disco while their parents went to the theatre. At the disco, there was a band and lots of people in costumes danced to their music. The musicians were in costumes too. It was very cool and exciting. Gita and Arun danced all evening and had a lot of fun.

9 STUDY SKILLS Lost and found

2 She guided the group of kids through the fields, but she didn't know the way.
3 "Do we turn left at the next road or do we turn right?"
4 Her phone was dead and the little kids in the group didn't have phones.
5 "We can stop here and wait for help or we can try to find the way back."
6 She hoped for a light or a sound and that's when she heard the noise.
7 She wasn't sure what it was, but she knew it came from the campsite.

◀)) **1** LISTENING **Interesting people**
02

Hörtext

Ruby	I think we're lucky this school year, Ellis. There are so many cool students.
Ellis	Yeah, it's great. School is a lot more fun when there are interesting kids around.
Ruby	Yeah, like Kisi. She's a lot of fun.
Ellis	Wait. I forget. Who is Kisi?
Ruby	She has long, straight, black hair that she wears in a ponytail.
Ellis	Does she sit next to you in English?
Ruby	Yes, that's her. She tells really funny jokes.
Ellis	Luis is like that too. He doesn't try to be funny, but he knows how to have a good time. I laugh a lot when he's around. You know Luis, right?
Ruby	Is Luis in our class?
Ellis	No, he isn't. I know him from the basketball team. He has short, black hair and wears glasses.
Ruby	Oh, him. He's really good at sports. Right?
Ellis	Yeah, that's Luis.
Ruby	Do you know Jayden? I think he's a friend of Luis's.
Ellis	Hm, Jayden. Let me think. What does he look like?
Ruby	He's short and he has long, curly, blond hair.
Ellis	I think I know him. I tried to talk to him in the canteen one day, but he was very quiet.
Ruby	He doesn't talk much. We're in the computer club together. I like Jayden because he's always helpful and nice when I have computer problems. He's really good with computers.
Ellis	Oh, that's right, you're in the computer club. Do you know Vera? She has short, red hair and braces.
Ruby	Oh, sure, I know Vera. She sits with us in the canteen sometimes.
Ellis	I like her. She's so strong and confident. Did you know she likes climbing?
Ruby	Really? I'm not surprised.
Ellis	I remember that day in class when Jack was very unfriendly to the teacher and Vera told him to sit down and be quiet. I thought that was very brave.
Ruby	Yeah, she doesn't like it when people are unfair or mean.
Ellis	She told me she wants to be an activist one day.
Ruby	That's the perfect job for her!

💡

Die Aufgaben stehen in der Regel in der gleichen Reihenfolge, in
der die entsprechenden Stellen im Text vorkommen.

a)

Luis

Vera

Kisi

Jayden

b)

1 next to • **2** jokes • **3** try • **4** basketball • **5** quiet • **6** helpful • **7** confident • **8** activist

2 READING **A normal hero**

		true	false
1	After the film, Lyle wanted to be a hero like Zap and Astrogirl.	✓	
2	The man fell because Lyle's bike was in his way.	✓	
3	Lyle called 999 because he wanted to help the man.	✓	
4	The police told Lyle that he was in trouble.		✓
5	Lyle's parents found out what happened when they read the newspaper.	✓	
6	Lyle knew that he was a superhero, but he didn't want to tell his parents.		✓

3 WORDS **Parts of the body**

1 eye • **2** nose • **3** head/hair • **4** ear • **5** face • **6** arm • **7** hand • **8** leg • **9** ankle • **10** foot

4 WORDS **Describing people and things**

1 kind • **2** untidy • **3** unfair • **4** unhappy • **5** confident • **6** honest • **7** dangerous

5 LANGUAGE **Meeting a sports hero**

a)

1 Did you go ...?
2 Did you wear ...?
3 Did the school have ...?
4 ... I didn't.
5 ... I did.
6 ... they didn't.

b)

1 When did you learn ...?
2 Why did you become ...?
3 How did you get ready ...?
4 What did you do ...?

6 MEDIATION **Eine Klassenfahrt**

1 Yes, it was a class trip. They were away for four days.
2 Yes. The bus driver had long hair and sunglasses. He was also funny.
3 There was snow on the ground and it was sunny. It was perfect for skiing.
4 Yes, they did. They fell a lot and laughed a lot. But they also learned a lot.
5 Lea fell and hurt her ankle.
6 Jonas went too fast and hit him. Yusuf hurt his leg.

> Du muss nicht 1:1 übersetzen.
> • Sage es anders: Wenn du ein Wort nicht kennst, versuche es mit anderen Wörtern zu umschreiben.
> • Sage es kurz: Bilde kurze und einfache Sätze, um Fehler zu vermeiden.

7 WRITING **One of my friends**

Benutze die Checkliste um zu kontrollieren, ob du die Aufgabe erfüllt hast. Hast du etwas über die folgenden Themen geschrieben? Gib dir drei Punkte für jedes Thema, das du erwähnt hast.

Did you ...			✓
write about what the person looks like?	long/short • straight/curly • black/blond/dark/red • hair blue/brown/green • eyes braces • glasses		
write about the person's personality?	brave • clever • confident • cool • fair • friendly • funny • good at/with ... • helpful • honest • kind • polite • quiet • nice		
say how you met?	The first time we met was ... • I think we met at/when ... • We became friends when/after/ ...		
write about why you are happy to be friends with this person?	He/She	helps me • listens to me • never gets too angry/excited/stressed • teaches me a lot	
	We	have fun together • laugh a lot • like the same things • share everything	
write 60 words or more?			
		Total: _____ / 15	

(Lösungsbeispiel)

One of my friends is Herr Werner. He's the trainer for our football club. He has short, blond hair. He often wears a football shirt with the name of our club on it. He's always very fair and he's really funny. He's also a clever trainer. I think we met on my first day at football. I like him because he always stays calm when we play a game and he makes us feel like winners when we win — and when we don't win.

8 STUDY SKILLS **Finding the right words**

1 invitation • **2** climber • **3** neighbours • **4** arrival • **5** helpful • **6** ill • **7** scary

1 LISTENING Planning a visit

Hörtext

Yusuf	I can't wait, Selma!
Selma	Yes! I can't remember the last time I visited you and your family.
Yusuf	I think it was last summer.
Selma	I don't think so, Yusuf. Last summer you came here.
Yusuf	Oh, you're right! But it was some time last year. How are you going to get here this time?
Selma	I'm travelling by train. It arrives at 7 p.m. on Friday.
Yusuf	Great. We can come and get you from the train station.
Selma	Cool!
Yusuf	Let's make some plans, Selma. On Friday evening Dad is going to cook chicken curry for dinner. After that we can play video games. Is that OK?
Selma	Sure!
Yusuf	What about on Saturday? Any ideas?
Selma	Yes. I'd like to check out that zip wire at Brighton Beach.
Yusuf	The Beach Zip? That's really fun.
Selma	What's more exciting – the zip wire or the Brighton Viewing Tower?
Yusuf	Oh, the zip wire is more exciting.
Selma	Then let's go on the zip wire.
Yusuf	OK, cool. We can do that in the morning when it isn't so full of people.
Selma	And after that, if it's OK, I'd like to walk around Brighton Palace Pier.
Yusuf	That's perfect, because my favourite fish and chips shop is near the pier. We can have some lunch there after we walk around a bit.
Selma	I love fish and chips.
Yusuf	This place makes the best in the world.
Selma	Great! But let's do something in the afternoon that doesn't cost money.
Yusuf	I agree. Hey, I have a great idea!
Selma	What is it?
Yusuf	I'm going to give you a walking tour. Brighton is full of amazing street art and I can show you where the best street art is.
Selma	Oh, fun! I want to take pictures of it all.
Yusuf	We're going to be tired after that, cousin.
Selma	Yeah – but the best kind of tired. What are we going to do on Sunday?
Yusuf	I have one or two ideas. First, we …

a)

b)

		true	false
1	Selma's last visit to Brighton was last summer.		✓
2	Selma is going to arrive in Brighton on Friday at 7 in the evening.	✓	
3	Yusuf's mum is going to make chicken curry for dinner.		✓
4	The zip wire at Brighton Beach is more exciting than the i360 tower.	✓	
5	Yusuf knows a place where they can eat lunch.	✓	
6	Selma wants to do something in the afternoon that's free.	✓	

2 READING Film reviews

1 The main character in Never Stop is **Lottie**.
2 Never Stop takes place in **East London**.
3 The Superlatives are a **superhero** family.
4 If you like funny films, *The Superlatives – Home Sweet Home* is the best film to see.
5 Play for your life is one of the best sci-fi films of the year because it has amazing special **effects**, weird **characters** and a **clever** story.
6 The film with the best rating is *Never Stop*.
7 The film with the worst rating is *The Superlatives*.

Je mehr englische Texte du liest, desto größer wird dein Wortschatz und desto schneller und besser verstehst du Texte.

3 WORDS **An amazing evening**

1 theatre • 2 creative • 3 energetic • 4 artists • 5 created • 6 prepared

4 WORDS **Music, films and shows**

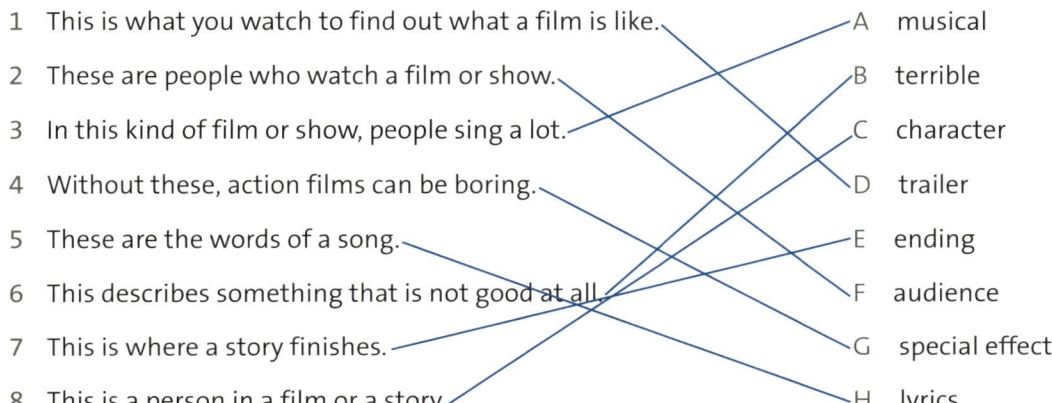

1 This is what you watch to find out what a film is like. — A musical

2 These are people who watch a film or show. — B terrible

3 In this kind of film or show, people sing a lot. — C character

4 Without these, action films can be boring. — D trailer

5 These are the words of a song. — E ending

6 This describes something that is not good at all. — F audience

7 This is where a story finishes. — G special effects

8 This is a person in a film or a story. — H lyrics

5 WORDS **Finding Amelia**

1	2	3	4
E	F	C	B
5	6	7	8
A	G	D	H

6 LANGUAGE **What do you think?**

2 I think that thrillers are **more exciting than** action films. But sci-fi films are **the most exciting**.

3 I think cartoons are **funnier than** game shows. But comedies are **the funniest**.

4 I think sushi is **better than** pizza. But fish and chips are **the best**.

5 I think musicians are **cooler than** footballers. But actors are **the coolest**.

7 LANGUAGE **Activity week**

a)

1 are going to have
2 isn't / is not going to be
3 are going to do
4 aren't / are not going to have
5 are going to teach
6 is going to explain

b)

1 Are we going to do …? Yes, you are.
2 Are you going to open …? No, I'm/we're not.
3 When is Mr Shaw going to give his talk?
4 How are we going to get …?

8 MEDIATION **A noisy cafe**

(Lösungsbeispiel)

1 ... they're / they are (even) louder...
2 ... they're / they are not as loud as here.
3 ... it's very exciting.
4 ... it's too busy, with too many cars, buses and people.
5 ... we're going to go to the British Museum.
6 ... we're going to take the bus to Covent Garden.

> Achte auf kulturelle Unterschiede: Versetze dich in dein Gegenüber hinein und überlege, was für diese Person wichtig ist, um die Situation oder die Inhalte verstehen zu können.

9 WRITING **It's going to be cool!**

Benutze die Checkliste um zu kontrollieren, ob du die Aufgabe erfüllt hast.

Did you ...		
tell your friend that they talked about Sports Week?	Yes, we did / they did. • we/they talked about ...	_____ / 3
write about what, when and where for at least three activites?	at the sports field • in the assembly hall • in the Gym • at 12:45	*3 Punkte pro Aktivität = 9 Punkte gesamt* _____ / 9
answer your friend's question about choosing tennis together?	We can... • I like your idea. • How about we... • Let's do...	_____ / 3
		Total: _____ / 15

(Lösungsbeispiel)

Yes, they talked about Sports Week next week. It's going to be cool! On Monday I'm going to play golf at 2:30 at the sports field. I can't wait! On Tuesday I'm going to play table tennis level 1 at 12:45 in the assembly hall. Would you like to do football level 2 at 12:45 on Wednesday at the sports field? And I like your idea too! Tennis is in the timetable. We can play tennis level 1 on Tuesday at 2:15. Does that sound good?

10 STUDY SKILLS **That's my opinion**

1 my opinion • 2 that isn't true • 3 I agree • 4 You're right • 5 do you think • 6 think

1 LISTENING Celebrating with friends

Hörtext

Myra   Hi Danny!

Danny   Hey, Myra. You're wearing white clothes. That's great!

Myra   They're not going to be white for very long – not after the fun starts. I'm so excited!

Danny   You really are. Have you ever been to the festival before?

Myra   No, I haven't. This is my first time.

Danny   You're going to love it. The others are going to meet us in the park at one o'clock, before the music starts.

Myra   Right. When does the fun start with all the colours?

Danny   That comes later.

Myra   Oh, OK. Tariq has just texted me. He is going to bring a few bottles of lemonade.

Danny   That's perfect. It's going to be hot today.

Myra   And I talked to Jenna this morning. She wants to bring some biscuits.

Danny   Sounds good.

Myra   So, Danny, do you have the … you know?

Danny   Of course! That's the most important thing! It's in my rucksack.

Myra   Cool! Here comes the bus. Let's go!

Danny   This looks like a good place. I brought a picnic blanket to sit on.

Myra   Good idea. Well, we're on time. Where is everybody?

Danny   Somebody is texting me. … It's Tariq. He's going to be a bit late.

Myra   Oh, my phone. … Oh no, Jenna can't come. Her mum is sick and needs her help.

Danny   That's a shame. That means no biscuits.

Myra   Well, did you think I wouldn't bring anything?

Danny   What's that in that box, Myra?

Myra   Ta-da!

Danny   Ahh, biscuits! Hey, look over there. Do you see that? The musicians are getting ready.

Myra   I can't wait to dance. And look, here comes Tariq!

Danny   Hi, Tariq.

Tariq   Hi, sorry I'm late, but look what I've got — nice and cold.

Myra   Ah, the lemonade. Well done. Show him what you have in your rucksack, Danny.

Danny   Yep. Look at these.

Tariq   What are they?

Danny   They're packets powder in lots of different colours! I've brought some for everybody!

Myra   Look at those colours! Now we can celebrate Holi!

All   Yeah! Woo-hoo!

> Beim Hören: Versuche, zunächst grob zu verstehen, worum es in dem Text geht. Konzentriere dich auf die Schlüsselwörter aus der Aufgabenstellung.
> Achte auf den Kontext. Manchmal gibt der Text weitere Informationen, die klar machen, was gemeint ist. So kannst du Wörter erschließen, die du nicht kennst.

a)

1 Notting Hill Carnival 2 Holi ✓ 3 Guy Fawkes Night 4 Eid al-Fitr

b)

1 Myra is wearing ...
- [ ] a) clothes in rainbow colours.
- [ ] b) jeans and a T-shirt.
- [✓] c) white clothes.

2 The friends agree to meet ...
- [ ] a) at the bus stop at one o'clock.
- [ ] b) in the park at two o'clock.
- [✓] c) in the park at one o'clock.

3 Tariq texts them to say he's going to bring ...
- [✓] a) lemonade.
- [ ] b) some biscuits.
- [ ] c) a picnic blanket.

4 Danny and Myra arrive there by ...
- [ ] a) train.
- [✓] b) bus.
- [ ] c) bike.

5 Jenna can't come because ...
- [ ] a) she's sick.
- [✓] b) her mum is sick.
- [ ] c) she has to do chores.

6 Danny has ... in his rucksack.
- [ ] a) a costume.
- [ ] b) a box of biscuits.
- [✓] c) packets of powder in different colours.

2 READING Hello from Brighton

		true	false
1	Frida is on holiday in Brighton with her family.		✓
2	Aisha's brother Amir is 15, like Frida.		✓
3	Frida feels like she hasn't been anywhere yet.		✓
4	She was worried on her first day at school, but everybody was nice to her.	✓	
5	School in Brighton is sometimes hard for Frida.	✓	
6	Frida celebrated Eid al-Fitr together with Aisha's family.	✓	
7	Aisha's parents prepared all the food.		✓

3 WORDS **Guy Fawkes Night**

1 knock
2 somebody
3 still
4 scared
5 put on
6 fireworks
7 terrible

4 WORDS **My favourite food**

2 a piece of cheese
3 a packet of biscuits
4 a bag of onions
5 a box of chocolates
6 a bottle of orange juice

5 LANGUAGE **Anything you want**

Mayil Can I have (1) **some** cola please, Dad?
Dad No, sorry Mayil, you can't have (2) **any** cola, but you can have (3) **some** tea or juice.
Mayil Can I have (4) **some** cake?
Dad There isn't (5) **any** cake. Would you like (6) **some** biscuits?
Mayil I don't want (7) **any** biscuits, thanks. I'll just have (8) **some** tea.

6 LANGUAGE **An invitation**

1 Everybody • 2 everywhere • 3 anything • 4 everything • 5 someone

7 LANGUAGE **Party time**

a little – a few

- **a little** bedeutet **ein wenig, ein bisschen, etwas**.

  We need **a little** time/milk/music.
  Wir brauchen **etwas** Zeit/Milch/Musik.

- **a few** bedeutet **ein paar, einige**.
  Du verwendest **a few** mit dem Plural von Nomen.

  We need **a few** minutes/bottles/songs.
  Wir brauchen **einige** Minuten/Flaschen/Songs.

Noah Mum, (1) **a few** guests have just arrived!
Mum Oh dear. I need (2) **a little** more time.
Noah Would you like (3) **a little** help?
Mum Yes, thank you, Noah. Can you put (4) **a few** strawberries on the cake?
Noah Of course. It should only take (5) **a few** minutes.
Mum Great! Then we're ready!

8 LANGUAGE **My favourite things**

Vor dem Lesen: Schaue dir die Überschrift und die Bilder an, die zum Text gehören. Sie geben dir bereits Hinweise über den Inhalt des Textes.

a)

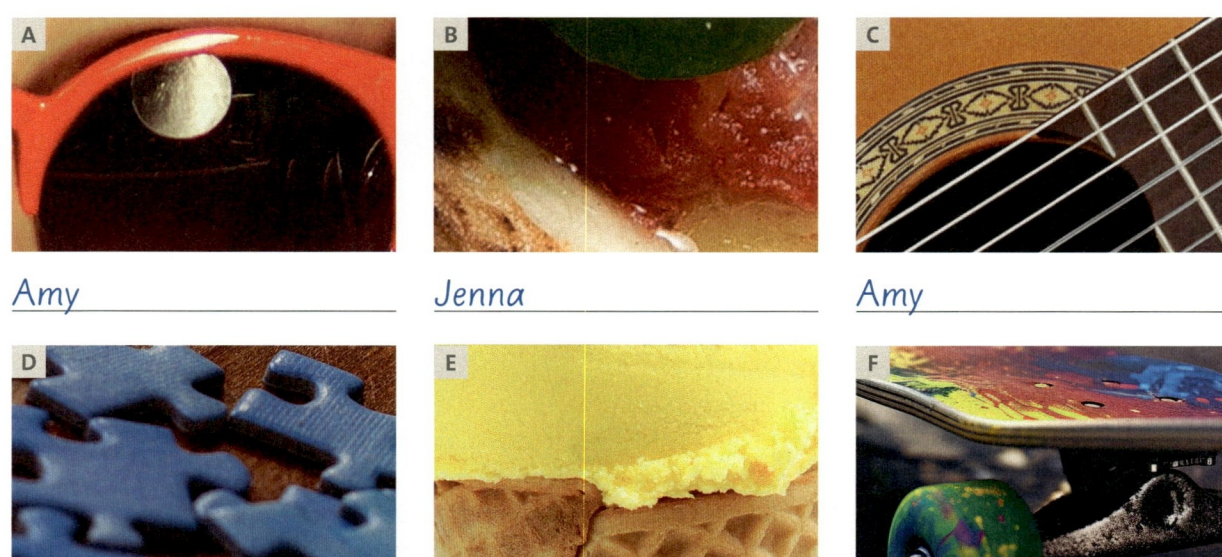

Amy

Jenna

Amy

Karim

Karim

Jenna

b)

1 One of Jenna's favourite things ... (C) is something her friends have too.
2 She loves pizza ... (D) that doesn't have meat on it.
3 Karim likes big jigsaw puzzles ... (E) because they're hard.
4 Amy bought one of her favourite things ... (A) when she was on holiday.
5 She's not very good at it, but ... (B) she still loves playing her guitar.

9 MEDIATION **A special day**

1 Sie feiern Saint Patrick's Day. Die Leute tragen grün, und es gibt Paraden/Umzüge.
2 Robyn sagt, dass sie Irland feiern.
3 Es gibt eine Parade, Kunst, Märkte und irische Musik überall.
4 Sie war mit Freunden unterwegs. Sie haben ihre Gesichter grün angemalt und haben lustige Kostüme angezogen. Sie schickt uns Fotos.

Checkliste Mediation

✓ nur die wichtigen Infos weitergeben
✓ unbekannte Wörter umschreiben
✓ kürze und einfache Sätze verwenden
✓ auf Pronomen achten

10 WRITING A birthday celebration

Benutze die Checkliste um zu kontrollieren, ob du die Aufgabe erfüllt hast. Gib dir drei Punkte für jede Frage, die du mit „ja" beantwortest. Wenn du die Aufgabe nur zum Teil erfüllt hast, gib dir zwei Punkte.

Did you ...		✓
write about all three things listed under "today"?	• arrive at Auntie Nicky's house • surprise Granny with birthday cake • have big family dinner	
use simple past to write about the things that happened "today"?	We **arrived** ... at 11 am. In the afternoon we **surprised** ... Later we **had** a big dinner.	
write about all three things listed under "tomorrow"?	• go for a walk with Granny Ann • Dad makes fish and chips for lunch • Dad and I drive to Brighton	
use going to-future to write about the plans for "tomorrow"?	I**'m going to go** for a walk ... in the morning. Dad**'s going to make** ... for lunch. At 4 p.m. we**'re going to drive** ...	
use a least 2 words or phrases from the word box?	birthday cake • chicken / lamb / pork • to arrive early / on time • candles • to give sb. a present • to have sth. for dinner • to surprise sb. • to thank sb.	

Total: _____ / 15

(Lösungsbeispiel)

Hey Allie, it's going great. We arrived on time at 11 a.m. *We had a fun day. In the afternoon we* surprised Granny Ann with a birthday cake. There were a lot of candles! After that we gave her presents and she thanked everybody. *Later we* had a big family dinner. We had lamb and it was delicious!
Tomorrow morning, I'm going to go for a walk with Granny Ann. It's something she and I like doing together. *At 12 o'clock, Dad* is going to make fish and chips for lunch. *At 4 p.m.* Dad and I are going to drive back to Brighton.

11 STUDY SKILLS A Chinese celebration

(Lösungsbeispiel)

CHINESE NEW YEAR
- clean and decorate at home
- special foods
- fireworks and parades

Beachte bei einer Präsentation am Computer:
• Wähle ein einfaches Folienlayout.
• Beschränke dich auf wenig Text.
• Wähle nur ein Bild pro Folie.

Speaking

🔊 05 1 MONOLOGUE A celebration (Unit 1, Unit 4)

(Lösungsbeispiel)

I remember I celebrated the end of the last school year with the kids in my class. We had a big picnic. Our teacher was there and a lot of parents were there too. I went there with my dad. The celebration was in a city park. Everybody brought some kind of food or drink. I brought some cheese sandwiches and a big bowl of strawberries. The picnic was a lot of fun. We played football and we sang karaoke. For me the karaoke was the best. I didn't like the football so much because it was too hot on that day.

🔊 06 2 MONOLOGUE Giving directions (Unit 3)

(Lösungsbeispiel)

Turn right on Castle Road,
then turn left on Victoria Street. Go past the museum and
take the next left on Barley Road. Then take the second left
and you'll see the street market on your left.

Alle Lösungsbeispiele aus diesem Kapitel kannst du aus deiner Cornelsen Lernen App abspielen.

🔊 07 3 MONOLOGUE An interesting person (Unit 2, Unit 5)

(Lösungsbeispiel)

My Aunt Lisa is a really interesting person. She has brown hair that's long and curly, and her eyes are brown too. She's short, like my dad. Aunt Lisa is clever and creative and very funny. She's a cook in a restaurant, so she's good at preparing food, but she's also good at thinking fast. I like Aunt Lisa because she's very funny and she's always friendly and kind to me and to other people.

🔊 08 4 DIALOGUE A good teacher (Unit 2)

(Lösungsbeispiel)

Partner A What do you think? What makes a good teacher?
Partner B I think a good teacher has to be very funny and clever.
Partner A Well, I think it's important that a teacher is friendly.
Partner B I don't agree. It's important to be kind, but it's not important to be friendly.
Partner A Why do you think that a teacher doesn't have to be friendly?
Partner B Because students often don't work hard when the teacher is too friendly.
Partner A OK. A teacher doesn't have to be friendly, but he or she needs to be kind and fair.
Partner B Yes, I agree. And I like teachers who are hard-working. What do you think?
Partner A Yes, that's important.
Partner B Great. Then we agree on three things. It is important for a good teacher to be hard-working, kind and fair.
Partner A Yes.

🔊 09 5 DIALOGUE Making plans (Unit 3)

(Lösungsbeispiel)

Partner A Let's do something together this weekend!
Partner B OK, great! What are we going to do?
Partner A On Saturday we could go to the street market and shop for clothes.
Partner B That's a good idea, but I'd like to go to the trampoline park too. They have a special price this weekend. It's only £3. We could go after the street market. It stays open until 6 p.m.
Partner A OK, that's fine. So first we're going to go to the street market in the morning. Then we can go to the trampoline park in the afternoon. What about after that?
Partner B What about the skatepark? There's a skate competition at 3 p.m. We could go there a bit later.

Partner A   I don't really want to go there after trampolining. We're going to be tired. Let's do something quieter. What about the comic book club? That's in the evening. It's a lot of fun. And this week it's all about superheroes, my favourite.

Partner B   I like that idea! Superheroes are so cool.

Partner A   Great. Hey, on Sunday afternoon some school friends are going to have a beach clean-up party. I'd like to go. What about you?

Partner B   That sounds good! Let's do it!

6   Dialogue   In a clothes shop (Unit 5)

(Lösungsbeispiel)

Partner A   Hello, can I help you?

Partner B   Yes, please. I'm looking for some trainers.

Partner A   We have these blue trainers here.

Partner B   Those are nice. I'd like to try them on.

Partner A   What size are you?

Partner B   I need size 40.

Partner A   Right. Here's a size 40. You can try them on here.

Partner B   Thank you. I like these!

Partner A   I think they're your size.

Partner B   I'll take them. How much are they?

Partner A   They're 45 pounds. Would you like to pay by card or cash?

Partner B   I'll pay by card.

Partner A   OK. ... Here's your card.

Partner B   Thank you.

Partner A   You're welcome. Goodbye!

Let's talk (Schulbuch, S. 195–199) enthält Wendungen für wichtige Situationen, wie z.B.: Sich verabreden und etwas planen.

Unit 5 Getting ready for the future

🔊
11

1 LISTENING I want to be a ...

Hörtext

Dad	How was school today, Luis?
Luis	It was OK. We had a guest speaker in our class – an architect. He talked to us about his job and what he does.
Mum	That sounds interesting. Do you think you'd like to be an architect?
Luis	Hm. I don't think so. But I know that Anna wants to be one. She had lots of questions for him.
Dad	Why does Anna want to be an architect?
Luis	She told me that she wants to design really cool houses.
Dad	It's a hard job, but Anna is creative. I think she'll be successful.
Mum	What do your other friends want to be?
Luis	Nick wants to be a cook and have his own restaurant.
Mum	That's great! I'm not surprised. Nick is very hard-working.
Luis	He's just discovering cooking. He helps his parents in the kitchen a lot and he loves it.
Dad	You should be more like Nick, Luis, and help in the kitchen.
Luis	Ha-ha. I've heard that the restaurant business is very busy and hard.
Dad	Yes, you have to be energetic and hard-working.
Luis	Oh, and Melanie wants to be a footballer. That's not surprising. It's all she talks about.
Mum	If she's good, she'll make a lot of money.
Dad	But she has to be confident and strong. It's a hard sport and women footballers still don't earn as much as the men. What about you, Luis? Have you thought about what you want to be?
Luis	Yes, Sure.
Mum	When you were little you wanted to be a firefighter.
Luis	That was a long time ago, Mum. Now I want to be a nurse.
Mum	Interesting. Why a nurse?
Luis	It looks like an exciting job. And every day you're helping and saving people.
Dad	Being a nurse is an important job. You have to be calm and kind because you're working with people who need your help.
Luis	Do you think I'll earn enough money?
Mum	Maybe not as much as an architect or a footballer, but I'm sure you'll be fine.

a)

Anna: D architect
Nick: C cook
Melanie: A footballer
Luis: B nurse

b)

1 design; creative • **2** hard-working; restaurant • **3** confident; strong • **4** calm; kind

2 READING What do you do with your pocket money?

	true	false
1 Manu spends some of his pocket money online.	✓	
2 He puts some money in a savings account.		✓
3 When Jenny goes out, she spends only half of her pocket money.	✓	
4 Jenny's rabbits sometimes get something special to eat.	✓	
5 Dylan is creative.	✓	
6 His hobby doesn't cost much.		✓
7 Eve often spends too much on clothes.		✓
8 Eve doesn't like spending money on concerts.		✓

3 WORDS Chores

4 WORDS Jobs in the family
1 G vet
2 A firefighter
3 E programmer
4 F shop assistant
5 B hairdresser
6 H writer
7 C mechanic

5 WORDS **My favourite aunt**

1 look forward to · **2** gamer · **3** solve · **4** owner · **5** earns · **6** successful · **7** made up

6 LANGUAGE **Seeing into the future**

1 'll/will work · **2** 'll/will share · **3** won't/will not go · **4** will walk · **5** will call · **6** will be ·
7 won't/will not earn · **8** won't/will not know · **9** 'll/will remember · **10** 'll/will get · **11** will move

7 LANGUAGE **When I'm thirty-five**

I will / I'll be an artist.
I will not / won't work in an office.
I will / I'll teach kids to draw and paint.
I will / I'll live in a house on the beach.
I will / I'll have two cats.
I still will not / won't like doing chores.

8 LANGUAGE **At the market**

1   Luca and I went to the street market on Saturday. /
    On Saturday Luca and I went to the street market.
2   Luca often buys clothes.
3   I usually get some delicious street food.
4   I spent almost five pounds at a fish-and-chips stand this time. / This time I spent almost five pounds
    at a fish-and-chips stand.

9 MEDIATION **In a shop**

1   Do you have rain jackets?
2   She would like a green one.
3   S ist too small for her. Do you have a blue one in size M?
4   She likes the blue jacket (more than the green one). How much is it?
5   She'll take it.
6   She would like to pay by card.

10 WRITING A big change

Benutze die Checkliste um zu kontrollieren, ob du die Aufgabe erfüllt hast.

Did you …			
use all the notes from the list?	- Mum > better job - Me > a new adventure - miss Brighton	- my new school > be good - kids and teachers > be nice - not live near the sea	*1 Punkt pro Notiz = 6 Punkte* _____ / 6
use the will-future at least 3 times?	I'll / It'll / They'll / We'll … • I/it/we/they won't …		_____ / 6
Use at least 3 words or phrases from the box?	I think / hope … • I'm sure … • It's a shame that … • Let's … • move • stay in contact • look forward to … • sad • strange • different • interesting • …		_____ / 3
		Total:	_____ / 15

(Lösungsbeispiel)

Hi guys,

I have some sad news. My mum has a new job in Leeds, so we're going to move there in the summer. Mum will have a better job, so that's good. For me it will be a new adventure. I'm sure some things will be different and other things will be the same. But I'll miss Brighton! I hope that my new school will be good and that the kids and teachers there will be nice. Leeds will be very different, I'm sure. It's a shame that we won't live near the sea. Let's stay in contact, guys! I look forward to texting and having video calls often with you.

Bye for now,

Manu

Ein Text ist noch nicht fertig, wenn du ihn zu Ende geschrieben hast. Du solltest ihn noch mehrmals durchlesen bzw. in Partnerkorrektur durchlesen lassen.

Im *Skills file* (Schulbuch, S. 169) findest du wichtige Informationen zum Überprüfen und Verbessern von Texten.

11 STUDY SKILLS Check your writing

a)

1 Does the email start and end correctly?   yes ☐ no ☑

2 Is the email friendly and personal?   yes ☑ no ☐

b)

Hi Rosie
How are you? I hope that <u>you enjoying</u> the summer break.
Our new house is great and I've already met a few nice
<u>neahbours</u>, but I miss <u>brighton</u>. Here I don't know anybody,
so it's boring. And I don't feel comfortable riding my bike
here because <u>I the city don't know.</u>
I'm looking <u>forword</u> to starting school. Then I'll make some
friends and I won't feel so alone. I've already <u>saw</u> my new
school.
I miss you, Rosie! Let's have a video chat soon.
<u>Manu</u>

you are enjoying

neighbours

Brighton

I don't know the city.

forward

seen

Bye (for now)/See you.

Unit 4
Celebrate!

🔊 04

1 LISTENING **Celebrating with friends** _____ / 7 ▶ SB, pp. 98–99

Read the tasks carefully. Then listen to some friends who meet for a celebration. *Lies die Aufgaben sorgfältig durch. Dann höre den Freunden zu, die sich für eine Feier treffen.*

a) **What are they celebrating? Tick (✓) the right picture.** *Was feiern sie? Markiere (✓) das richtige Bild.* *(1 Punkt)*

1 Notting Hill Carnival   2 Holi   3 Guy Fawkes Night   4 Eid al-Fitr

b) **Listen again. Tick (✓) the correct answer – a), b) or c).**
Höre noch einmal zu und markiere (✓) die richtige Antwort – a), b) oder c). (6 Punkte)

1   Myra is wearing ...
- [ ] a) clothes in rainbow colours.
- [ ] b) jeans and a T-shirt.
- [ ] c) white clothes.

2   The friends agree to meet ...
- [ ] a) at the bus stop at one o'clock.
- [ ] b) in the park at two o'clock.
- [ ] c) in the park at one o'clock.

3   Tariq texts them to say he's going to bring ...
- [ ] a) lemonade.
- [ ] b) some biscuits.
- [ ] c) a picnic blanket.

4   Danny and Myra arrive there by ...
- [ ] a) train.
- [ ] b) bus.
- [ ] c) bike.

5   Jenna can't come because ...
- [ ] a) she's sick.
- [ ] b) her mum is sick.
- [ ] c) she has to do chores.

6   Danny has ... in his rucksack.
- [ ] a) a costume
- [ ] b) a box of biscuits
- [ ] c) packets of powder in different colours

▶ Check 🔽

2 READING **Hello from Brighton** _____ / 7

▶ SB, pp. 100–101

Frida is a German exchange student who is living in Brighton for three months. She has written to her English class in Germany. Read her email. *Frida ist eine deutsche Austauschschülerin, die für drei Monate in Brighton wohnt. Sie hat eine Mail an ihre Englischklasse in Deutschland geschrieben. Lies ihre Mail.*

to	birgit.bauer@example.edu
from	frida.wilhelm@example.net

Hi everybody,

I arrived here two weeks ago and so much has happened already! I'm staying with the Khan family and they are really nice. Their daughter Aisha is 15, like me, and her brother, Amir, is two years younger than me.

I really like Brighton. It only takes a few minutes by bike from the Khans' house to the beach. That's so cool! They've already taken me to a lot of cool places. I told Aisha that I feel like I've been everywhere. She said, "You haven't seen anything yet!"

At school it was a bit weird on the first day. I felt nervous, but my class teacher, Mr Whittaker, welcomed me and made some jokes. He said, "You speak English better than I do!" We laughed about that. Everyone in my class was really friendly too. But school hasn't been easy. Some days it feels like I haven't learned anything.

Last weekend was the end of Ramadan, so the family celebrated Eid al-Fitr. Aisha's cousins and aunts and uncles were there – and everyone arrived with something delicious to eat. There was music and dancing too. It was an amazing celebration! Check out this photo!

Bye for now,
Frida

True or false. Tick (✓). *Richtig oder falsch? Markiere (✓).*

		true	false
1	Frida is on holiday in Brighton with her family.		
2	Aisha's brother Amir is 15, like Frida.		
3	Frida feels like she hasn't been anywhere yet.		
4	She was worried on her first day at school, but everybody was nice to her.		
5	School in Brighton is sometimes hard for Frida.		
6	Frida celebrated Eid al-Fitr together with Aisha's family.		
7	Aisha's parents made all the food.		

▶ Check

3 Words **Guy Fawkes Night** _____ / 7

► SB, pp. 221–226

Tariq is describing an experience that he had. Complete his statement with the words from the box. _Tariq schildert ein Erlebnis. Vervollständige seine Ausssagen mit den korrekten Wörtern aus dem Kasten._

> fireworks • knock • put on • scared • somebody • still • terrible

It was Guy Fawkes Night and I was at home, waiting for my friend Alex. We wanted to go to a bonfire[1].

It was almost dark. There was a loud (1) _____ at our door. I opened the door

and (2) _____ with a Guy Fawkes mask on stood there and said nothing at all.

"Hello?" I said, but the person (3) _____ didn't answer. It was a really weird moment.

Then the person laughed and took off the mask. It was Alex! I laughed too. I didn't tell him that

he (4) _____ me. At the bonfire, Alex (5) _____ his mask again.

We stood and watched the fire. Then I heard loud noises. I looked up and saw (6) _____.

"Look!" I said, turning to Guy Fawkes. The mask didn't say anything. "Oh, stop being weird!" I said.

"Are you talking to me?" a girl asked from behind the mask. I heard Alex laughing further away.

It was (7) _____.

[1] **bonfire** _das (große Freuden-) Feuer_

4 Words **My favourite food** _____ / 5

► SB, p. 191

Ms Friedman has asked her class to say what their favourite food or drink is. Complete their statements with words from the two boxes. _Frau Friedman hat ihre Klasse gefragt, was ihr Lieblingsessen oder -getränk ist. Vervollständige die Aussagen der Klasse mit den Wörtern aus den beiden Kästen._

> a bag of • a bottle of • a box of • a dish of • a packet of • a piece of

+

> biscuits • cheese • chocolates • onions • orange juice • yoghurt

1 _a dish of yoghurt_____   4 _____

2 _____   5 _____

3 _____   6 _____

► Check

5 LANGUAGE Anything you want ____ / 8

► SB, p. 101, p. 179

Mayil and her dad are getting something to eat and drink at the Holi celebration. Complete their dialogue with *some* and *any*. *Mayil und ihr Papa holen sich etwas zum Essen und Trinken beim Holi-Fest. Vervollständige ihren Dialog mit* some *und* any.

Mayil	Can I have (1) _____ cola please, Dad?
Dad	No, sorry Mayil, you can't have (2) _____
	cola, but you can have (3) _____ tea or juice.
Mayil	Can I have (4) _____ cake?
Dad	There isn't (5) _____ cake.
	Would you like (6) _____ biscuits?
Mayil	I don't want (7) _____ biscuits, thanks.
	I'll just have (8) _____ tea.

! *Some* (einige, etwas) verwendest du:
– in bejahten Aussagen
– in Fragen, wenn du um etwas bittest oder wenn du jemandem etwas anbietest.

Any (kein, keine, keinen) verwendest du in verneinten Sätzen.

6 LANGUAGE An invitation ____ / 5

► SB, p. 109, p. 181

Noah has sent a party invitation to his friends. Complete the invitation with the words in the box. *Noah hat seinen Freundinnen und Freunden eine Party-Einladung geschickt. Vervollständige die Einladung mit den Worten im Kasten.*

anything • everybody • everything • everywhere • someone

Hey (1) _____,

We're finally in our new house! It's still a bit messy – there are boxes (2) _____ – but I love this place. We want to celebrate next Saturday and you're invited! You don't have to bring (3) _____. We're going to organize (4) _____ – drinks, food, music and games. If you'd like to bring (5) _____ with you, like a friend or a parent, that's cool. Hope to see you, Noah P.S. My new address is 24 Watson Road.

7 LANGUAGE Party time ____ / 5

► SB, p. 102, p. 179

Complete the sentences with *a little* or *a few*. *Vervollständige die Sätze mit* a little *oder* a few.

Noah	Mum, (1) _____ guests have just arrived!
Mum	Oh dear. I need (2) _____ more time.
Noah	Would you like (3) _____ help?
Mum	Yes, thank you, Noah. Can you put (4) _____ strawberries on the cake?
Noah	Of course. It should only take (5) _____ minutes.
Mum	Great! Then we're ready!

! zählbare Nomen → a few
unzählbare Nomen → a little

► Check

8 READING **My favourite things** _____ / 11

▶ SB, pp. 110–111, p. 163

A blogger has asked her readers to name two of their favourite things. Read these answers. *Eine Bloggerin hat ihre Leserinnen und Leser nach ihren zwei Lieblingssachen gefragt. Lies die Antworten.*

> *One of my favourite things is my skateboard. I ride it almost every day. Some of my friends have skateboards too, so we go skateboarding a lot together. Pizza is the other thing I love. I don't eat meat, so I always have vegetarian pizza. It's my favourite! ~ Jenna*

> *I'm a big fan of jigsaw puzzles. They're never boring for me. The ones with 1000 pieces are my favourites. They're not easy and that's why I like them. Mango ice cream is my other favourite thing. I like almost any kind of ice cream, but mango is really the best. ~ Karim*

> *Last year on holiday I bought some cool sunglasses. They're one of my favourite things. Sometimes, when it's cloudy, I still wear them! My other favourite thing is my guitar. It's acoustic and it sounds really nice. I'm not very good at playing it, but I'm learning. ~ Amy*

a) Match the close-up photos with the correct person. Write the person's name under each picture. *Ordne die Nahaufnahmen der richtigen Person zu. Schreibe den Namen der Person unter das Bild. (6 Punkte)*

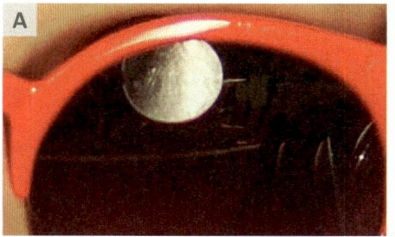

_____

_____

_____

_____

_____

_____

b) Match (1–5) with the correct ending (A–F). There's one extra ending. *Verbinde (1–5) mit den Satzenden (A–F). Es gibt ein zusätzliches Satzende. (5 Punkte)*

1 One of Jenna's favourite things ...

2 She loves pizza ...

3 Karim likes big jigsaw puzzles ...

4 Amy bought one of her favourite things ...

5 She's not very good at it, but ...

A when she was on holiday.

B she still loves playing her guitar.

C is something her friends have too.

D that doesn't have meat on it.

E because they're hard.

F but he likes mango the most.

▶ Check

9 MEDIATION **A special day** _____ / 4

► SB, pp. 98–101, p. 164

The Irish exchange student who stayed with you
last year has sent your family a postcard from Cork.
Your parents have some questions about it. Read her
postcard and answer your parents' questions.

_Die irische Austauschschülerin, die letztes Jahr bei dir
gewohnt hat, hat deiner Familie eine Postkarte aus
Cork geschickt. Deine Eltern haben Fragen dazu.
Lies ihre Postkarte und beantworte die Fragen deiner Eltern._

POSTCARD

Hi everybody,
Happy Saint Patrick's Day!
I wanted to share with you the
amazing time I've had here today.
March 17th is a special day. Of course, it's
a celebration of Saint Patrick, but we really
just celebrate Ireland! Here in Cork it's the
biggest day of the year. Lots of people come
here for the parade, but there's also art,
markets and Irish music everywhere. I've
been out with my friends all day. We
wanted to have a little fun, so we put on
green make-up and funny hats.
I can send you photos!
Bye, Robyn

For Correspondence

Familie Kramer
Kleeblattstr. 14
48143 Münster
Germany

For Address Only

1   Mutter: Das ist lieb von Robyn. Was ist das Besondere am 17. März?

Du: Sie feiern _____ .

2   Vater: Aber es geht nicht nur um diesen Sankt Patrick, oder?

Du: Robyn sagt, _____

_____ .

3   Vater: Also bei ihr in Cork ist es ein großes Event. Das habe ich kapiert. Was passiert denn?

Du: _____

_____ .

4   Mutter: Ich möchte hören, was Robyn an dem Tag gemacht hat. Was hat sie geschrieben?

Du: _____

_____ .

► Check ⬇

10 WRITING **A birthday celebration**   ____ / 15   ▶ More help, p. 78   ▶ SB, pp. 100–103, pp. 108–109

Ben and his dad have travelled to Bristol to celebrate his grandma's 70th birthday. Ben's friend Allie texts him late that evening. Read Ben's diary notes and answer Allie's questions. You can use the ideas in the box or your own. *Ben ist mit seinem Vater nach Bristol gereist, um den 70. Geburtstag seiner Großmutter zu feiern. Bens Freundin Allie schreibt ihm spät am Abend eine SMS. Lies Bens Tagebucheintrag und beantworte Allies Fragen. Du kannst die Ideen im Kasten oder deine eigenen verwenden.*

Granny Ann's birthday	
today	tomorrow
11 a.m. – arrive at Aunt Nicky's house	10 a.m. – go for a walk with Granny Ann
2 p.m. – surprise Granny with a birthday cake	12 a.m. – Dad makes fish and chips for lunch
7:30 p.m. – have big family dinner	4 p.m. – Dad and I drive to Brighton

> to arrive early / on time • birthday cake • chicken / lamb / pork • candles • to give sb. a present •
> to have sth. for dinner • to surprise sb. • to thank sb.

Hey Ben, how's it going in Bristol? When did you arrive? Was it an exciting day? Tell me what you did! ✓

Hi Allie! It's going great. We arrived ____
____
____

We had a fun day. In the afternoon we ____
____
____

Later we ____
____
____ ✓

Sounds cool! What's your plan for tomorrow? What time are you going to drive back? ✓

Tomorrow morning, I'm going to ____
____
____

At 12 o'clock, Dad ____
____
____

At 4 p.m. ____
____
____ ✓

▶ Check 📱

11 STUDY SKILLS A Chinese celebration _____ / 4   ▸ SB, pp. 114–115, pp. 165–166

Emily is giving a presentation about a tradition that her family celebrates. Read her statement and use the information to make a slide. Make the notes on the slide short and clear. *Emily hält eine Präsentation über eine chinesische Tradition, die ihre Familie feiert. Lies ihre Aussage und benutze die Informationen, um eine Folie zu erstellen. Mache die Notizen kurz und klar.*

Chinese New Year celebrates the new year in the traditional Chinese calendar. It starts in January or February and goes for 16 days. At home, people clean and decorate their houses with red for good luck. Families enjoy special foods during this time and every food brings something good, like a happy family or a long life. In the city, there are lots of fireworks and parades with loud music to scare away bad luck. The highlight of the parade is often a dragon.

_____

• _____

• _____

• _____

Bereich	Aufgabe	erreichte Punktzahl		🤩	😎	🥴	😭
listening	1	_____ / 7		7	6–5	4	3–0
reading	2	_____ / 7 ⎫	_____ /18	18–16	15–13	12–9	8–0
	8	_____ / 11 ⎭					
words	3	_____ / 7 ⎫	_____ /12	12–11	10–8	7–6	5–0
	4	_____ / 5 ⎭					
language	5	_____ / 8 ⎫					
	6	_____ / 5 ⎬	_____ /18	18–16	15–13	12–9	8–0
	7	_____ / 5 ⎭					
mediation	9	_____ / 4		4	3	2	1–0
writing	10	_____ / 15		15–14	13–11	10–8	7–0
skills	11	_____ / 4		4	3	2	1–0
Gesamt		_____ / 78		78–70	69–55	54–39	38–0

▸ Check ⬇

Speaking

1 MONOLOGUE A celebration (Unit 1, Unit 4)

▶ SB, pp. 14–17, pp. 100–103

Think of the last time you celebrated something. Maybe it was a birthday (yours or someone else's) or a holiday (e.g. Christmas). What can you remember about it? *Überlege, wann du zuletzt etwas gefeiert hast. Vielleicht war es ein Geburtstag (von dir oder einer anderen Person) oder ein Feiertag (z.B. Weihnachten). Woran kannst du dich erinnern?*

Make notes about …
— what and where you celebrated
— who you celebrated with
— what you brought with you or prepared

— what kind of activities there were
— what you enjoyed
— what you didn't like

You can use these pictures for ideas:

Talk about the celebration. You can start like this:
I remember I celebrated …
I went to … at …
I was with …
The celebration was in/at …
I brought/prepared a/some …

Höre dir die Lösungsbeispiele an und achte nicht nur auf den Inhalt, sondern auch auf Aussprache und Intonation.

▶ Check ⬎

2 MONOLOGUE Giving directions (Unit 3)

► SB, pp. 80–81, pp. 218–219

You are on holiday with your family. You're staying in a hostel in Castle Road. At breakfast another visitor who doesn't have his phone with him asks you for directions to the street market in Blackwell Road. Look at the map. Draw the way from the hostel to the street market. Then give the man directions from the hostel to the street market.

Du bist mit deiner Familie im Urlaub. Ihr wohnt in einem Hostel in der Castle Road. Beim Frühstück fragt dich ein anderer Besucher, der sein Handy nicht dabei hat nach dem Weg zum Straßenmarkt in der Blackwell Road. Schaue die Karte an. Zeichne den Weg vom Hostel zum Straßenmarkt. Beschreibe dann dem Mann den Weg vom Hostel zum Straßenmarkt.

Nimm dich beim Üben auf. Danach kannst du kontrollieren, ob du wirklich alles gesagt hast, was du sagen wolltest.

You can use the phrases in the box and your own ideas:

Turn left / right at (the) …
Go across / down / past / through / up (the) …
Go straight on at (the) …
When you come to / see (the) …, then …
… the first / second / … street on your left / right …

Turn right on Castle Road, then turn left on …

► Check

3 MONOLOGUE An interesting person (Unit 2, Unit 5)

▶ SB, pp. 40–43, p. 142, p. 186

Talk about a person who you like. It can be somebody you know, somebody famous, or maybe a character from a book, film or TV series. The words and phrases in the box will help you. Circle the words you want to use. *Sprich über eine Person, die du magst. Es kann eine Person sein, die du persönlich kennst, jemand berühmtes oder vielleicht ein Charakter aus einem Buch, Film, oder einer TV Serie. Die Wörter und Sätze in der Box werden dir helfen. Umkreise die Wörter, die du nutzen möchtest.*

a) **Think about what he or she looks like. Think about the person's**
   – hair
   – eyes
   – size

black • blond • brown • curly • long • red • short • straight
blue • blue-green • brown • dark • eyes • glasses
short • tall

b) **Think about his or her personality.**

brave • clever • confident • creative • fair • friendly • funny • kind • practical

c) **Think about what the person does and what he or she is good at.**

actor • artist • bus driver • cook • dancer • footballer • gamer • hairdresser • mechanic • nurse • programmer • student • teacher • writer	
He/She is good at... maths • sports • listening • drawing • solving problems	He/She is good with ... children • animals • computers

d) **Talk about this person and what you like about them. Use the words you circled in a), b) and c).**

> *My Aunt Lisa is a really interesting person. She has brown hair that's long and curly, and her eyes are brown too. She's short, like my dad. Aunt Lisa is ...*

▶ Check

4 DIALOGUE A good teacher (Unit 2)

▶ SB, pp. 42–45, p. 186, p. 198

🔊
08

It's the end of the school year and you and your partner are talking about the teachers who you thought were good. Look at the list below. What makes a good teacher? Tick three things that you think are important. *Es ist das Ende des Schuljahres und du und dein Partner oder deine Partnerin sprecht über die Lehrkräfte, die ihr gut fandet. Schaut euch die Liste unten an. Was macht eine gute Lehrkraft aus? Hake drei Dinge ab, die du wichtig findest.*

☐ clever   ☐ good with technology
☐ confident   ☐ good at listening
☐ fair   ☐ kind
☐ friendly   ☐ smart
☐ funny

Talk with your partner. Agree on three things that are important for a good teacher.
You can use the ideas in this box or your own:
Sprich mit deinem Partner oder deiner Partnerin. Einigt euch auf drei Dinge, die für eine gute Lehrkraft wichtig sind. Ihr könnt die Ideen aus der Box oder eure eigenen Ideen verwenden:

> I think a good teacher has to be ... • has to be / have ... •
> I like teachers who / that are ... • I think / For me it's important that a teacher is ... •
> That's true, but I think it's more important to be ... • I don't think a teacher has to be ... •
> I agree. • I don't agree.

You can start like this:

Partner A: *What do you think? What makes ...?*

Partner B: *I think ...*

Partner A: *Well, I think it's important that ...*

Partner B: *I don't agree. He or she has to be ...*

Partner A: *Why do you think that ...?*

Partner B: *Because ...*

💡 Wenn du Dialoge übst, finde ein Gegenüber, mit dem du zusammen üben kannst, am besten jemand aus deinem Englischkurs. Du kannst auch eine Freundin, einen Freund, oder jemanden aus deiner Familie, der Englisch spricht, bitten, mit dir Dialoge zu üben.

▶ Check

5 DIALOGUE **Making plans (Unit 3)**

▶ SB, pp. 74–75, p. 167, p. 196

🔊
09

You and your partner want to do something together this weekend. Look at the ideas that you have noted down in your phone. *Du und dein Partner oder deine Partnerin wollen dieses Wochenende etwas gemeinsam unternehmen. Schau dir die Ideen an, die du in deinem Handy notiert hast.*

A
- Street market: shop for clothes
  Saturday, 9 a.m. – 4 p.m.
- Skatepark: skate competition
  Saturday, 3 p.m.
- Beach clean-up party with
  school friends
  Sunday, 3 p.m.

B
- Trampoline park: special price £3
  all weekend
  Saturday and Sunday,
  9 a.m. – 6 p.m.
- Comic book club: This week's
  topic is *Why we love superheroes*
  Saturday evening
- Bike tour by the beach,
  Sunday at 2 p.m.

Talk with your partner, share your ideas and find out about his or hers. Agree on three things that you'd like to do together. The phrases in the box will help you. *Sprich mit deinem Partner oder deiner Partnerin, teile deine Ideen und finde heraus welche Ideen er oder sie hat. Einigt euch auf drei Dinge, die ihr gerne gemeinsam machen würdet. Die Satzteile in der Box helfen dir.*

> I'd like to … • I (don't) really want to … • I have a good / better idea!
> Let's … • That's a good idea. • That's too … • We could … • What about a …? • What about you?

You can start like this:

Partner A: *Let's do something together this weekend!*

Partner B: *OK, great! What are we going to do?*

Partner A: *On Saturday we could …*

Partner B: *That's a good idea, but I'd like to …*

Partner A: *OK, that's fine. So first we're going to … . What about after that?*

 ▶ Check

6 DIALOGUE In a clothes shop (Unit 5)

► SB, pp. 137–139, p. 199

🔊 10

Work with a partner and agree on your roles – Partner A or Partner B. Then look at your role cards.

Arbeite mit einem Partner oder einer Partnerin. Einigt euch auf eure Rollen – Partner A oder Partner B. Schaut euch dann eure Rollenkarten an.

Partner A

You are a shop assistant in a clothes shop. Partner B is a customer in your shop. Help the customer choose and pay for one of the items above. You can use the phrases below or your own.

You start.

- *Hello, can I help you?*
- *What size ...?*
- *The changing rooms are ...*
- *I (don't) think it's your size.*
- *You look ...*
- *It is ... / They are ...*
- *Would you like to try on / look at ...?*
- *Would you like to pay by ...?*
- *You're welcome.*

Partner B

You are a customer in a clothes shop. Partner A is the shop assistant. You are shopping for one of the items in the illustrations above. You can use the phrases below or your own.

Partner A starts.

- *Yes, please.*
- *I'm looking for ... / Do you have ...?*
- *I need size ...*
- *I'd like to try it on. Where are the ...?*
- *I (don't) like ...*
- *How much is/are ...?*
- *That's fine. / Oh, that's too ...*
- *I think I'd like ... / I'll ...*
- *I'll pay by ...*
- *Thank you and ...*

When you are finished, swap roles.

This jacket is too big. These jeans are £30.

That jacket is your size. Those jeans are £50.

► Check

Unit 5
Getting ready for the future

1 LISTENING **I want to be a ...** _____ / 12

▶ SB, pp. 128–130, p. 193

a) Luis is talking with his parents during dinner about future jobs. Listen to their conversation. Look at the pictures and write the correct letter (A–D) and the job next to each name. *Luis spricht beim Abendessen mit seinen Eltern über zukünftige Berufe. Höre ihrem Gespräch zu. Schaue die Bilder an und schreibe den korrekten Buchstaben (A-D) und den Beruf neben jeden Namen. (4 Punkte)*

Anna: _____   Nick: _____

Melanie: _____   Luis: _____

b) Read the sentences carefully. Then listen again and complete the sentences with the correct words in the box. *Lies die Sätze sorgfältig durch. Höre dann noch einmal zu und vervollständige die Sätze mit den korrekten Wörtern aus dem Kasten. (8 Punkte)*

> calm • confident • creative • design • hard-working •
> kind • restaurant • strong

1 Anna wants to _____ houses. She'll be succsessful because she's

  _____.

2 Nick is very _____ – he wants to have his own _____.

3 Melanie can do well, but she has to be _____ and _____.

4 Luis will help people in his job if he is _____ and _____.

2 READING What do you do with your pocket money? _____ / 8   ▶ SB, pp. 136–137

Read the answers to this question that some students in Brighton have given. Then complete the exercise. *Lies die Antworten auf diese Frage, die einige Schülerinnen und Schüler aus Brighton gegeben haben. Vervollständige dann die Übung.*

Manu

Sometimes I buy sweets or snacks, or I buy something for a friend. I also like to shop for used comics and video games online. But I save some of my money too. Every week I put a few pounds in a piggy bank in my room. Maybe in the future I'll buy something bigger with the money.

Jenny

"Save a little, spend a little" – that's what my mum says. I get pocket money every week. I always put half of it in my savings account. Then I can't spend it on anything unimportant. I like to buy treats for my two rabbits and sometimes I go to the cinema with friends. At the moment I'm saving for a new phone.

Dylan

I spend most of my pocket money on my hobby. My friends think it's weird, but I like building things that fly – especially small planes and drones. It's cool to try to create my own. But it's an expensive hobby – there's always something more that I need. I'm lucky that my uncle helps me. He has the same hobby!

Eve

Sometimes I buy clothes with my pocket money, but only when there's something that I really want. It's nice to have things, but I want to spend my money on cool activities and events like concerts, sports, rides and museums. It's just more fun. So I try to stay away from shopping centres.

Tick (✔) true or false. *Hake ab (✔), richtig oder falsch.*

		true	false
1	Manu spends some of his pocket money online.		
2	He puts some money in a savings account.		
3	When Jenny goes out, she spends only half of her pocket money.		
4	Jenny's rabbits sometimes get something special to eat.		
5	Dylan is creative.		
6	His hobby doesn't cost much.		
7	Eve often spends too much on clothes.		
8	Eve doesn't like spending money on concerts.		

▶ Check 🔖

3 WORDS **Chores** _____ / 6

► SB, pp. 136–137, p. 194

Deval is telling a friend why he was late to the skatepark. Put the pictures in the right order.

Deval erzählt einem Freund, warum er zu spät zum Skatepark gekommen ist. Bringe die Bilder in die richtige Reihenfolge.

After breakfast I tidied my room, as always. I was ready to go after that, but then my mum asked me to take the dog out. "It won't take long," she said. So I got ready to take our dog Snuffy outside. Then my dad said, "Please take out the rubbish on your way". So I did that. Later, when Snuffy and I came back, my dad was outside by the car. He said, "Deval, please also …", and I said "…wash the car?". And he said, "It won't take long." After I did that, I thought I was finished. But my mum called from inside the house. She asked me to empty the dishwasher. So I went inside and did that. Then I asked, "Can I go to the skatepark now?" She said, "Yes … after you set the table for lunch. It won't take long."

4 WORDS **Jobs in the family** _____ / 7

► SB, pp. 128–130, p. 228

Felicia loves talking about the people in her family and their interesting jobs. Match each person with the right job (A-H). There is one job that doesn't match. *Felicia liebt es, über die Leute in ihrer Familie und ihre interessanten Jobs zu reden. Verbinde jede Person mit dem richtigen Job (A-H). Es gibt einen Job, der nicht passt.*

1 Mum often tells us about the different animals she's helped. _____

2 Dad works at strange times of day and night, helping fight fires. _____

3 Dad's sister, Aunt Bess, is always working on a new software. _____

4 Uncle Will enjoys helping customers in the clothes shop. _____

5 Grandma Lily still likes cutting hair after all these years. _____

6 Cousin Jesse wrote a short story about Grandma. _____

7 Uncle Vince knows how to keep the cars in our family running well. _____

A firefighter
B hairdresser
C mechanic
D nurse
E programmer
F shop assistant
G vet
H writer

► Check

5 WORDS **My favourite aunt** _____ / 7 ▶ SB, pp. 227–233

Felicia is still talking about her family. Complete her statements with the words from the box. There are two words that you don't need. *Felicia redet immer noch über ihre Familie. Vervollständige ihre Aussagen mit den Wörtern aus dem Kasten. Es gibt zwei Wörter, die du nicht brauchst.*

> cook • earns • gamer • look forward to •
> made up • owner • prediction • solve • successful

I always (1) _____ visiting Uncle Will and Aunt Bess.

Aunt Bess knows that I'm a (2) _____ ,

so we talk about video games and coding. As a programmer, she often has

to (3) _____ difficult software problems. She's also a

video game business (4) _____ .

She (5) _____ a lot of money from her game *Future*

World. It's the most (6) _____ video game of the year.

That's why I've (7) _____ my mind: I want to be a programmer just like Aunt Bess.

Erklär-film

6 LANGUAGE **Seeing into the future** _____ / 11 ▶ SB, pp. 131–132, p. 182

Isla is sitting in a cafe one day when a strange woman sits down at her table and tells her that she can see into Isla's future. Complete her predictions with *will* or *'ll* and *won't*. *Isla sitzt eines Tages in einem Café als sich eine fremde Frau zu ihr setzt und ihr sagt, sie könne in Islas Zukunft sehen. Vervollständige ihre Vorhersagen mit* will *oder* 'll *und* won't.

When you are 25 you (1) _____ (work)

in an office. Also, you (2) _____ (share)

a flat with a friend who takes very long showers.

This (3) _____ (not go) well. One day a grey cat

(4) _____ (walk) into your flat and

become your best friend. You (5) _____ (call) him Mr Nibbles.

At work your boss (6) _____ (be) horrible, and you (7) _____

(not earn) much money. You (8) _____ (not know) what to do with your life.

Then you (9) _____ (remember) that you wanted to become a vet.

After a lot of studying and hard work, you (10) _____ (get) an exciting job

in a vet clinic. You and Mr Nibbles (11) _____ (move) to a nice new house

with a cat door.

▶ Check

7 LANGUAGE **When I'm thirty-five** _____ / 6

► SB, pp. 131–132, p. 182

Erklär-film

Deval's class has made posters about their future lives when they're thiry-five years old. Look at the pictures and phrases on Deval's poster. Write his sentences, use the will-future. *Devals Klasse hat Poster über ihr zukünftiges Leben im Alter von fünfunddreißig Jahren erstellt. Schau dir die Bilder und Sätze auf Devals Poster an. Schreibe seine Sätze. Nutze das will-future.*

When I'm thirty-five ...

be an artist

live in a house by the sea

not work in an office

have two cats

teach kids to draw and paint

still not like doing chores

_____

_____

_____

_____

_____

_____

8 LANGUAGE **At the market** _____ / 4

► SB, p. 137, p. 182

Put the sentence parts in the correct order. *Bringe die Satzteile in die richtige Reihenfolge.*

1 the street market / went to / on Saturday / Luca and I /.

_____

2 buys / often / clothes / Luca /.

_____

3 get / delicious street food / I / some / usually /.

_____

4 almost five pounds / I / at a fish-and-chips stand / this time / spent /.

_____

► Check

9 MEDIATION **In a shop** _____ / 6   ► SB, pp. 137–138, p. 164

You're on holiday and you're looking around in a clothes shop when you hear an older German woman talking. She's having trouble communicating with the shop assistant. You offer to help. Complete the dialogue. *Du bist im Urlaub und du schaust dich in einem Klamottenladen um. Du hörst eine ältere deutsche Frau, die Schwierigkeiten hat, mit der Verkäuferin zu kommunizieren. Du bietest deine Hilfe an. Vervollständige den Dialog.*

Woman: Das ist sehr lieb von dir. Könntest du bitte die

Verkäuferin fragen, ob sie Regenjacken hat?

You: Excuse me, please. (1) _____

_____ ?

Assistant: Yes, of course. We have them in different colours: green, blue, black and red.

You: Ja, hat sie - und zwar in verschiedenen Farben: grün, blau, schwarz und rot.

Woman: Ich würde gerne eine grüne Jacke haben.

You: (2) _____

Assistant: Green is a popular colour. We only have a few in size S.

You: Grün ist sehr beliebt, sagt sie. Sie haben nur noch einige in S.

Woman: Schade. Das ist mir zu klein. Ob sie eine blaue in Größe M hat?

You: (3) _____

Assistant: Let me see. Here's a blue one in size M.

You: Das ist eine blaue Jacke in M.

Woman: Schön! Die blaue Jacke gefällt mir auch besser als die grüne. Was kostet sie?

You: (4) _____

Assistant: This one costs £43.95.

Woman: Das habe ich schon verstanden. Das ist ein wenig teuer, aber ich brauche eine gute Regenjacke. Ich nehme sie.

You: (5) _____

Assistant: Great. Would she like to pay by card or cash?

You: Möchten Sie Bar oder mit Karte zahlen?

Woman: Ich möchte mit Karte bezahlen.

You: (6) _____

► Check

10 WRITING **A big change** _____ / 15

► More help, p. 79 ► SB, pp. 140–141

Manu is moving with his family from Brighton to Leeds in the summer. His mum has a new job there. He is writing an email to some friends to share the news and his hopes and predictions for the future. Help him write his email. Manu's notes and the words and phrases in the box will help you.

Manu zieht im Sommer mit seiner Familie von Brighton nach Leeds. Seine Mutter hat dort einen neuen Job. Er schreibt eine E-Mail an einige Freunde, um ihnen die Nachricht sowie seine Hoffnungen und Vorhersagen mitzuteilen. Helfe ihm, seine E-Mail zu schreiben. Manus Notizen und die Wörter und Phrasen im Kasten werden dir helfen.

– Mum > better job	– my new school > be good
– Me > a new adventure	– kids and teachers > be nice
– miss Brighton	– not live near the sea

I'll / It'll / They'll / We'll … • I/it/we/they won't … • I think / hope … • I'm sure … • It's a shame that … • Let's … • move • stay in contact • look forward to … • sad • strange • different • interesting • …

!

Mit dem _will-future_ sagst du, was in der Zukunft wahrscheinlich geschehen wird. Die Sätze beginnen oft mit _I think, maybe, I'm sure._ Bilde das _will-future_ mit _will_ und dem Infinitiv. _I think we'll be good friends._

Hi guys,

I have some sad news. My mum has a new job in Leeds, so we're going to move there in the summer.

Mum will _____

_____

_____

_____

_____

_____

_____

_____

_____

_____

_____

_____

► Check

11 STUDY SKILLS Check your writing _____ / 9

► SB, p. 144, p. 169

Manu is in his new home in Leeds. Read his email to his friend Rosie in Brighton.
Manu ist in seinem neuen Zuhause in Leeds. Lies seine E-Mail an seine Freundin Rosie in Brighton.

a) Tick (✓) yes or no. *Hake ab (✓) ja oder nein. (2 Punkte)*

   1   Does the email start and end correctly?   yes ☐   no ☐

   2   Is the email friendly and personal?   yes ☐   no ☐

b) **Improve the underlined parts.** *Verbessere die unterstrichenen Teile. (7 Punkte)*

Hi Rosie
How are you? I hope that <u>you enjoying</u> the summer break.
Our new house is great and I've already met a few nice
<u>neahbours</u>, but I miss <u>brighton</u>. Here I don't know anybody,
so it's boring. And I don't feel comfortable riding my bike
here because <u>I the city don't know.</u>
I'm looking <u>forword</u> to starting school. Then I'll make some
friends and I won't feel so alone. I've already <u>saw</u> my new
school. I miss you, Rosie! Let's have a video chat soon.
<u>Manu</u>

Bereich	Aufgabe	erreichte Punktzahl	🤩	😎	🤔	😭
listening	1	_____ / 12	12–11	10–9	8–6	5–0
reading	2	_____ / 8	8	7–6	5–4	3–0
words	3	_____ / 6				
	4	_____ / 7 } _____ /20	20–18	17–14	13–10	9–0
	5	_____ / 7				
language	6	_____ / 11				
	7	_____ / 6 } _____ /21	21–19	18–15	14–11	10–0
	8	_____ / 4				
mediation	9	_____ / 6	6	5	4–3	2–0
writing	10	_____ / 15	15–14	13–11	10–8	7–0
skills	11	_____ / 9	9–8	7–6	5	4–0
Gesamt		_____ / 91	91–82	81–64	63–46	45–0

► Check ↻

More help

▶ Unit 1, page 12

8 WRITING **Gita and Arun in Edinburgh** _____ / 15 ▶ SB, pp. 28–29

Look at the pictures. Then write the story about this sister and brother on their family holiday. Write about 80 words or more. Use the simple past. The words in the box can help you. *Schaue die Bilder an. Schreibe dann die Geschichte dieser Geschwister in dem Familienurlaub. Schreibe etwa 80 Wörter oder mehr. Benutze das simple past. Die Wörter im Kasten können dir helfen.*

arrived • station • got off

got • family room • four beds

festival • saw • poster

bought • cheap • costumes

excited • costumes • disco

wore • danced • had fun

Their train arrived at the station in Edinburgh and Gita and Arun _____

_____

At McPurdy's Hostel, _____

Later the family walked around in the city and _____

_____

They went to a second-hand clothes shop and _____

That evening, Gita and Arun _____

_____

▶ Check ⤵

▶ Unit 2, page 19

7 WRITING **One of my friends** _____ / 15   ▶ SB, pp. 40–43, p. 186

Look at the online post about someone's friend. Write a post about one of your friends. *Schaue den Online-Beitrag über einen Freund von jemandem an. Schreibe einen Beitrag über eine Freundin oder einen Freund von dir.*

Write about:
– what he/she is like (looks, personality)
– how you met
– why you are happy to be friends with this person

Use the words in the box or your own. Write 60 words or more.

Schreibe über:
– *was für ein Typ er/sie ist (Aussehen, Persönlichkeit)*
– *wie ihr euch kennengelernt habt*
– *warum du froh bist, mit dieser Person befreundet zu sein*

Du kannst die Wörter im Kasten verwenden oder deine eigene. Schreibe 60 Wörter oder mehr.

evie_sundowner43

♥ ◯ ▽

evie_sundowner43 Ginny and I met at music school last year. She's so cool and she always listens to my ideas. We often write songs …

He/She has	long/short • curly/straight • black/blond/brown/red hair
	blue/brown/green/grey eyes
	glasses • braces
He/She is	brave • clever • confident • cool • creative • fair • funny • good at/with … • helpful • honest • kind • quiet • nice
He/She	helps me • like the same things I like • listens to me • never gets too angry/excited • teaches me a lot
We	have fun • laugh a lot • play … • talk about … • share everything

I want to tell you about my friend _____.

He/She has _____ hair and _____.

He/She is very _____ and _____.

We became friends when _____

_____

I like him/her because _____

_____.

When we're together, we _____

_____

▶ Check ↘

▶ Unit 3, page 27

9 WRITING **It's going to be cool!** _____ / 15   ▶ SB, pp. 72–75

You're texting with a classmate who wasn't at the school assembly today. Look at the timetable and answer her questions about Sports Week. Name at least three activities that you're going to do. For each activity write what, when and where. *Du schreibst eine SMS an eine Schulkameradin, die heute nicht bei der Schulversammlung war. Schaue den Zeitplan an und beantworte ihre Fragen zu Sports Week. Nenne mindestens drei Aktivitäten, die du tun wirst. Für jede Aktivität schreibe was, wann und wo.*

SPORTS WEEK			
	in the **ASSEMBLY HALL**	in the **GYM**	at the **SPORTS FIELD**
on MON	at 12:45 Sports Week assembly	1:00 Fun with gymnastics 2:30 Gymnastics level 1	1:00 Football level 1 2:30 Golf level 1
on TUES	at 12:45 Table tennis level 1 at 2:15 Table tennis level 2	12:45 Basketball level 1 2:15 Volleyball level 1	12:45 Cricket level 1 2:15 Tennis level 1
on WED	at 12:45 Judo level 1 at 2:15 Judo level 2	12:45 Volleyball level 2 2:15 Gymnastics level 2	12:45 Football level 2 2:15 Tennis level 2
on THURS	at 12:45 Boxing level 1 at 2:15 Boxing level 2	12:45 Basketball level 2 2:15 Gymnastics final	12:45 Cricket level 2 2:15 Cricket final
on FRI	at 12:45 Table tennis final at 2:15 Judo final	12:45 Basketball final 2:15 Volleyball final	12:45 Football final 2:15 Tennis final

Did they talk about Sports Week at the assembly today? What activities are you going to do? Hey, let's do an activity together! Maybe tennis, if it's in the timetable? ✓

I'm going to try Judo at 12:45 on Monday in the assembly hall.

Yes, they talked about Sports Week. _____

On Monday I'm going to _____

_____

On Tuesday _____

_____

Would you like to _____

_____?

And I like your idea! We can _____

_____

▶ Check ⤵

▶ Unit 4, page 59

10 WRITING **A birthday celebration** _____ / 15 ▶ SB, pp. 100–103, pp. 108–109

Ben and his dad have travelled to Bristol to celebrate his grandma's 70th birthday. Ben's friend Allie texts him late that evening. Read Ben's diary notes and answer Allie's questions. You can use the ideas in the box or your own. *Ben ist mit seinem Vater nach Bristol gereist, um den 70. Geburtstag seiner Großmutter zu feiern. Bens Freundin Allie schreibt ihm spät am Abend eine SMS. Lies Bens Tagebucheintrag und beantworte Allies Fragen. Du kannst die Ideen im Kasten oder deine eigenen verwenden.*

Granny Ann's birthday	
today	tomorrow
11 a.m. – arrive at Auntie Nicky's house	10 a.m. – go for a walk with Granny Ann
2 p.m. – surprise Granny with birthday cake	12 p.m. – Dad makes fish and chips for lunch
5:30 p.m. – have big family dinner	4 p.m. – Dad and I drive to Brighton

to arrive early / on time • birthday cake • chicken / lamb / pork • candles • to give sb. a present • to have sth. for dinner • to surprise sb. • to thank sb.

Hey Ben, how's it going in Bristol? When did you arrive? Was it an exciting day? Tell me what you did! ✓

Hey Allie! It's going great. We arrived _____

_____

We had a fun day. In the afternoon we surprised _____

_____

After that we gave her _____

_____

Later we _____

_____ ✓

Sounds cool! What's your plan for tomorrow? What time are you going to drive back? ✓

Tomorrow morning I'm going to go for a walk _____

_____

At 12 o'clock, Dad is going to _____

_____

At 4 p.m. we are _____

_____

_____ ✓

▶ Check 🔧

▶ **Unit 5, page 73**

10 WRITING **A big change** _____ / 15 ▶ SB, pp. 140–141

Manu is moving with his family from Brighton to Leeds in the summer. His mum has a new job there. He is writing an email to some friends to share the news and his hopes and predictions for the future. Help him write his email. Manu's notes and the words and phrases in the box will help you.

Manu zieht im Sommer mit seiner Familie von Brighton nach Leeds. Seine Mutter hat dort einen neuen Job. Er schreibt eine E-Mail an einige Freunde, um ihnen die Nachricht sowie seine Hoffnungen und Vorhersagen mitzuteilen. Helfe ihm, seine E-Mail zu schreiben. Manus Notizen und die Wörter und Phrasen im Kasten werden dir helfen.

– Mum > better job	– my new school > be good
– Me > a new adventure	– kids and teachers > be nice
– miss Brighton	– not live near the sea

I'll / It'll / They'll / We'll … • I/it/we/they won't … •
I think / hope … • I'm sure … •
It's a shame that … • Let's … •
move • stay in contact • look forward to … •
sad • strange • different • interesting •

 Mit dem *will-future* sagst du, was in der Zukunft wahrscheinlich geschehen wird. Die Sätze beginnen oft mit *I think, maybe, I'm sure.* Bilde das *will-future* mit *will* und dem Infinitiv. *I think we'll be good friends.*

Hi guys,

I have some sad news. My mum has a new job in Leeds, so we're going to move there in the summer.

Mum will _____

_____

I hope that my new school will be _____

_____

It's a shame that we won't _____

_____

Let's stay in contact, guys! I look forward to _____

_____

_____

Manu

▶ Check

Cover
Personen am Strand: Cornelsen/Anja Poehlmann; Strandhäuschen: Shutterstock.com/JoolsW

Illustrationen
Cornelsen/**Evelt Yanait, Advocate Art:** S. 7, S. 8, S. 9, S. 12, S. 14, S. 15, S. 16, S. 20, S. 22, S. 24, S. 25, S. 26, S. 31, S. 35, S. 49, S. 54, S. 62/m., S. 66, S. 69, S. 70, S. 71, S. 72, S. 75; Cornelsen/**Irina Zinner**: S. 29, S. 62/u., S. 77

Fotos
S. 1: Cornelsen/Inhouse/Anne Weingarten; **S. 2:** PEFC Deutschland e.V.; **S. 3**: Cornelsen/Anja Poehlmann; **S. 7**/1a+1b+4a: stock.adobe.com/RP; **S. 7**/4b: stock.adobe.com/Tarik GOK; **S. 8**/Emoji: Shutterstock.com/Yefym Turkin; **S. 11**: stock.adobe.com/David Matthew Lyons; S. 13: Shutterstock.com/Yefym Turkin; **S. 17**: Shutterstock.com/PeopleImages.com - Yuri A; **S. 18**: Shutterstock.com/Phovoir; **S. 19**: Shutterstock.com/SeventyFour; **S. 19**/Emojis: stock.adobe.com/mukhamad; **S. 20**/Emojis: Shutterstock.com/Yefym Turkin; **S. 21**/A: mauritius images/Mara Brandl/imageBROKER; **S. 21**/B: stock.adobe.com/Mark; **S. 21**/C: stock.adobe.com/chika_milan; **S. 21**/D: stock.adobe.com/Africa Studio; **S. 21**/E: stock.adobe.com/HildaWeges; **S. 21**/F: stock.adobe.com/Diana Vyshniakova; **S. 23**: stock.adobe.com/akkash; **S. 28**: Shutterstock.com/Yefym Turkin; **S. 31**/1a+1b+4a: stock.adobe.com/RP; **S. 31**/4b: stock.adobe.com/Tarik GOK; **S. 38**/A: mauritius images/Mara Brandl/imageBROKER; **S. 38**/B: stock.adobe.com/Mark; **S. 38**/C: stock.adobe.com/chika_milan; **S. 38**/D: stock.adobe.com/Africa Studio; **S. 38**/E: stock.adobe.com/HildaWeges; **S. 38**/F: stock.adobe.com/Diana Vyshniakova; **S. 42**/1: stock.adobe.com/Frank; **S. 42**/2: stock.adobe.com/IndiaPix; **S. 42**/3: stock.adobe.com/Paul Maguire; **S. 42**/4: Shutterstock.com/Fevziie; **S. 44**/A: stock.adobe.com/Анна Демидова; **S. 44**/B: stock.adobe.com/EnriqueMJ; **S. 44**/C: stock.adobe.com/Nikolai Sorokin; **S. 44**/D: stock.adobe.com/janzwolinski; **S. 44**/E: stock.adobe.com/Elenathewise; **S. 44**/F: stock.adobe.com/Alisa; **S. 45**: stock.adobe.com/Mirador; **S. 53**/1: stock.adobe.com/Frank; **S. 53**/2: stock.adobe.com/IndiaPix; **S. 53**/3: stock.adobe.com/Paul Maguire; **S. 53**/4: Shutterstock.com/Fevziie; **S. 55**/1: stock.adobe.com/MdHafizur; **S. 55**/2: stock.adobe.com/steftach; **S. 55**/3: Shutterstock.com/N Ahmad; **S. 55**/4: Shutterstock.com/art4you1; **S. 55**/5: Shutterstock.com/Adisa; **S. 55**/6: stock.adobe.com/Vector Nazmul; **S. 55**/o.r.: stock.adobe.com/POSMGUYS; **S. 57**/A: stock.adobe.com/Анна Демидова; **S. 57**/B: stock.adobe.com/EnriqueMJ; **S. 57**/C: stock.adobe.com/Nikolai Sorokin; **S. 57**/D: stock.adobe.com/janzwolinski; **S. 57**/E: stock.adobe.com/Elenathewise; **S. 57**/F: stock.adobe.com/Alisa; **S. 58**/m.: Shutterstock.com/Vector Tradition; **S. 58**/o.: stock.adobe.com/PeoplesDesignStudios; **S. 60**/Emojis: Shutterstock.com/Yefym Turkin; **S. 60**/o.l.: stock.adobe.com/Kiattisak; **S. 60**/o.r.: stock.adobe.com/Mirador; **S. 61**/m.l.: stock.adobe.com/Ncorp; **S. 61**/m.m.: stock.adobe.com/simona; **S. 61**/m.r.: stock.adobe.com/linortis; **S. 61**/u.l.: stock.adobe.com/ghazii; **S. 61**/u.m.: stock.adobe.com/Nicholas Felix/peopleimages.com; **S. 61**/u.r.: stock.adobe.com/Seventyfour; **S. 62**/o.: stock.adobe.com/SynthexUA; **S. 63**: mauritius images/Prostock-studio/Alamy Stock Photos; **S. 64**: stock.adobe.com/T Hover/peopleimages.com; **S. 65**: mauritius images/Caia Image; **S. 67**/A: stock.adobe.com/pilipphoto; **S. 67**/B: stock.adobe.com/Monkey Business; **S. 67**/C: stock.adobe.com/anandart; **S. 67**/D: stock.adobe.com/Halfpoint; **S. 68**/o.l.: stock.adobe.com/IndiaPix; **S. 68**/o.r.: stock.adobe.com/Woraphon; **S. 68**/u.l.: stock.adobe.com/alfa27; **S. 68**/u.r.: stock.adobe.com/mimagephotos; **S. 69**/u.: stock.adobe.com/Andrii Nekrasov; **S. 74**: Shutterstock.com/Yefym Turkin; **S. 76**/Emojis: stock.adobe.com/mukhamad; **S. 76**/o.: Shutterstock.com/SeventyFour